Your Divorce, Your Dollars:

Financial Planning Before, During, and After Divorce

Akeela Davis, CFP, RFP, PRP, CDS
Certified Divorce Specialist (Financial Planning)

Self-Counsel Press
(a division of)
International Self-Counsel Press
USA   Canada

Self-Counsel Press acknowledges the financial support of the Government of Canada through the Book Publishing Industry Development Program (BPIDP) for our publishing activities.

Printed in Canada.

First edition: 2003

Cataloging in Publication Data

Davis, Akeela
  Your divorce, your dollars: financial planning before, during, and after divorce / Akeela Davis.

  (Self-counsel reference series)

  1-55180-430-1

    1. Divorced people — Canada — Finance, Personal. 2. Divorced people — United States — Finance, Personal. 3. Divorce settlements — Canada. 4. Divorce settlements — United States. I. Title. II. Series.
HG179.D375   2003   332.024′0653   C2003-911246-2

The article from the Smart Marriages Archive, reproduced in the *Divorce Statistics Collection* by Eric Beauchesne, Southern News (Monday, December 20, 1999), that appears in Chapter 1 is used with permission.

Table 1 in Chapter 5 is from Divorce Pro software and is reproduced with permission of the College of Divorce specialists.

Self-Counsel Press
(a division of)
International Self-Counsel Press Ltd.

1704 N. State Street	1481 Charlotte Road
Bellingham, WA 98225	North Vancouver, BC V7J 1H1
USA	Canada

Contents

NOTICE TO READERS

Laws are constantly changing. Every effort is made to keep this publication as current as possible. However, the author, the publisher, and the vendor of this book make no representation or warranties regarding the outcome or the use to which the information in this book is put and are not assuming any liability for any claims, losses, or damages arising out of the use of this book. The reader should not rely on the author or the publisher of this book for any professional advice. Please be sure that you have the most recent edition.

Thank you to my husband, Michael, and children, Adam and Nyssa, for their patience and support.

Thank you to Janet Murphy, LLB, and Rhona Lichtenwald, LLB, for their help and feedback.

Introduction

Alas! How light a cause may move
Dissension between hearts that love!

— Thomas Moore (1779 – 1852)

Divorce, from the time you begin to consider it, to the time your divorce decree is issued, is a process full of loss. There is the loss of dreams, hope, and trust. There is the loss of self-esteem and confidence, the loss of a sense of security, as well as the potential loss of relationships with children, family, and friends. Is it any wonder that so few divorces are "amicable"?

During this time of immense emotional upheaval and the accompanying grieving, it is not surprising that your reasonableness is at stake. You are trying to come to grips with a new reality in your life. But at the same time, you are expected to make logical financial decisions that will affect you far into the future.

Compounding this problem is the fact that you may find yourself making crucial decisions without sufficient preparation, advice, or understanding. The whole area of divorce and family law operates in a very gray, subjective environment.

There are no hard and fast rules, and no absolutes. There is little consistency in the application of the laws from state to state or province to province.

In the past, divorce was a territory in which only lawyers operated. However, lawyers are schooled in law, not finance, and a lawyer is not trained to advise you as to how the financial decisions you make today will affect you tomorrow, let alone 10 or 20 years from now.

The objective of this book is to help you prepare financially for a separation, and to help you understand the potential consequences of the choices you may find yourself making.

The above statement may sound cynical — but only until you look at the statistics. The numbers are shocking. In the year 2000 alone, 2,376,000 Americans were married, and about 1,100,000 became divorced. In the same year, approximately 153,300 Canadians were married, and 70,200 became divorced.

Our decisions about money are very closely tied to our emotions. This book attempts to make you, the reader who may be contemplating divorce, aware of *some* of the emotional flashpoints and how these can affect you long after your divorce is finalized. Along the way, it will acquaint you with spending patterns and the effects these may have had on your marriage and could have on your divorce settlement; the language of separation and divorce, as well as the divorce process itself; the ins and outs of settlement negotiations and interim and final settlements; and methods for calculating your post-divorce expenses and income. It will also examine the important questions of whether to keep or give up the house; and the division of assets such as pensions, 401Ks, IRAs, and RRSPs. Finally, this book will examine life after divorce — or remarriage preparedness, as it is called: how a cohabitation agreement can help ensure your security and help you to deal with the financial issues of blended families.

Financial planning is not only an important aspect of divorce, but is also something that can help ease you into your new, post-divorce life. It pays to stay as calm as you can during this difficult time and make the best decisions possible for your future.

Marriage, Finance, and Divorce

Lovers' quarrels are not generally about money.
Divorce cases generally are.

— Mason Cooley (b. 1927), US aphorist

A large percentage of divorcing couples cited finances as one of the major areas of marital conflict. This is true for all income brackets. In her book *When Money is the Drug*, Donna Boundry states that two common money issues fuel most marital fights: the first is unmet expectations (see Chapter 8 for more discussion of this factor); the second is differing financial priorities. Ironically, most couples getting married, even for the second or third time, never discuss expectations or finances prior to the big day.

The psychological and emotional issues associated with money are numerous, and for the most part, lie outside the scope of this book. However, to illustrate potential problem behaviors associated with money in a relationship, I have broken down the behavior into two common patterns: spending profiles and risk profiles. It can be useful to have an understanding of these behaviors, because financial patterns that surfaced during your marriage can also influence the behavior of both you and your spouse during the divorce settlement negotiations. I will also suggest some strategies by which you may be able to make your path to a settlement somewhat smoother than it might otherwise be.

Spending Profiles

Spending profiles cover a wide spectrum of behavior. At one end of the scale is the ultra-saver; at the other, the ultra-spender. Fortunately, most of us fall somewhere in between these two extremes.

Saver  Spender

Savers

The saver profile is that of someone who lives very much in the future. Savers like to build their net worth so that they always have something saved for a rainy day. They certainly do not like living paycheck to paycheck. They buy less than what they can afford (that is, they live beneath their means). They use debt sparingly and only to acquire assets, then get rid of that debt as quickly as possible. Their assets (paid-off home and car, money in the bank) give them a tremendous sense of security. They usually portray a stable, solid existence.

Spenders

Spenders, however, live very much in the present. They want to experience today, because they may not be here tomorrow. Traveling and enjoying the best life has to offer in food, clothing, and activities are, for them, the things that make life worth living. Spenders live well beyond their means and use debt to make up the shortfall. They will have the high-ratio mortgage on the grand home and will obtain a new — but leased — Mercedes every two years. They appear exciting, fun loving, and are very confident that they can handle whatever the future brings.

Savers, spenders, and conflict

Given these profiles, it is not difficult to understand the conflict that arises when a spender marries a spender, or a spender marries a saver. The degree to which a couple will be able to resolve their financial problems depends on many factors, one of which is where each of them is on the saver/spender spectrum.

The saver/saver marriages, while they may have issues as to the degree and type of saving, usually experience the least amount of financial conflict.

In a spender/spender marriage, however, issues are usually about lack of money. Since both are spenders, the cash and credit available to meet family bills or to pursue more immediate material pleasures are in short supply. Because both parties are confident of their own ability to handle their debts, each will often blame the other for any money problems they may be experiencing. These couples are crisis driven.

The third type of union is the spender/saver marriage, and that pairing is a minefield just waiting for someone to take a wrong step. The issues in this type of marriage involve necessity versus luxury, saving for the future versus living for the moment, and stability versus fun. Quite often, the very characteristics that attracted each member of such a couple to the other are what will cause the most strife between them. The stability of the saver is now viewed as dullness or miserliness. The fun-loving spender is viewed as wasteful and irresponsible. Each one's financial behavior threatens the basic emotional needs of the other. The inability of both to empathize and relate usually leads to divorce.

Risk Profiles

Risk profiles are similar to, but also quite different from, spending profiles. Risk and spending profiles may combine to form a completely different behavior than either alone would indicate. Risk profiles can be illustrated by looking at how an individual views insurance (a defensive action) and investments (an offensive action) as part of his or her overall financial security, and may be recognized as follows:

Risk Profile	Insurance Characteristics	Investment Characteristics
Ultra-conservative	• Lots of insurance • Lowest deductibles	• Likes to have large amounts of cash in the bank • Does not like any debts • Prefers solid income investments • Lacks diversification
Conservative	• Enough insurance • Not the highest deductible	• Likes blue-chip investments • Debts only against assets • Accepts prudent investment mix
Moderate	• Somewhat inadequate insurance • Mid to high deductibles	• Likes a mix of income, blue-chip, and growth investments • Committed to paying off non-asset debts quickly • Will use prudent tax shelters
Aggressive	• Little or no insurance • Highest deductible, if there is any insurance	• Speculator • Excessive debts • High-risk tax shelters • Prefers equity to income investments • Lacks diversification

Risk profiles and conflict

Just as in the saver/spender spectrum, partners with dramatically different risk profiles may experience more conflict in their marriages than those with similar profiles.

Even the members of saver/saver marriages can come into conflict when the risk profiles of the individuals are very different. If one member of a couple has an ultra-conservative risk profile and the other has a moderate- or high-risk profile, conflict may arise regarding where and how their savings are invested.

Sometimes, one partner may feel pushed into a category where he or she does not feel he or she belongs simply to offset the perceived risks taken by the other partner. Very seldom is this issue openly discussed, but the underlying resentment it causes is added to existing conflict. It can become very nasty indeed.

It is possible for couples with different profiles to resolve their financial disputes and create a workable solution. However, to accomplish this, the couple must assess their financial compatibility early in the relationship, identify potential conflict areas, and be committed to developing solutions to meet each partner's needs.

Spending Profiles, Risk Profiles, and Divorce

Sadly, more often than not, couples are not even aware of their personal money motivations, and during the separation and divorce process, these same patterns will come into play.

For instance, if you are a saver and find yourself having to come up with spousal support payments each month, you may not want to support what you see as your spender partner's extravagant lifestyle. Alternatively, if you are an ultra-conservative person, you may feel the need for a large settlement in order to feel secure, and your soon-to-be ex-partner most likely will totally disagree. Or, if your partner is a saver and you are the spender, he or she may be unwilling to split assets, as he or she sees the accumulation as belonging only to him or her. Look at the following example:

Matt and Jane got married right after university. They were married for 22 years. Matt was a good-time guy who loved to take vacations, buy a new vehicle every few years, and eat out. Matt was obviously the spender in the couple. Jane, while she went along with Matt in most things, needed to have some security. She insisted they contribute equal amounts to retirement investments every year. Matt invested all his money in technology stocks in 1999. Jane had a conservative, balanced portfolio.

The major asset to be split during their divorce was their retirement investments. As a result of the prolonged market downturn, Jane's investment was worth considerably more than Matt's.

Jane was adamant that she should not have to split her funds with Matt. She contended that since they invested the same amounts, but his reckless behavior caused his losses, she did not have to compensate him. She lost a costly fight, and the bitterness that resulted from that conflict poisoned all their subsequent dealings.

In many cases, a divorcing couple will need the assistance of a third party to reach a settlement that is truly acceptable to them both.

Professional Help

If you are considering separation and divorce, consider also creating a professional team to help you through the process. The amount you spend on this team may cost you far less in the long run than a poorly thought-out and emotionally motivated settlement would.

First of all, you will need a good lawyer for legal advice. Most cases that end up in court long after the divorce is over are the product of poorly written agreements. Your lawyer can help you make certain that the language of your agreement contains no hidden surprises and can help you drastically reduce the chances of your agreement being challenged due to imprecise wording or illegal clauses.

You may need a psychologist or counselor (often called divorce coaches) as well to help you deal with the emotional issues of the divorce, so that you can move forward with your life or put together a parenting plan. In addition, if you and your ex-spouse are of the saver/spender type or have vastly different risk profiles, you can benefit immensely by involving a third party whose job it is to help you understand each other's point of view and motivations — and thereby help you stay out of court.

A certified divorce specialist (that is, a financial planner with special training in divorce issues) can also be of great assistance. They model settlement offers so that you can see the potential long-term inpact. A certified divorce specialist can help you understand the financial impact of any divorce settlement on both your current and future lifestyle by helping you determine such issues as whether or not you can afford to keep the house and the tax implications of various settlement proposals.

If you consider that lawyers are not trained to give financial advice or deal with emotions; that psychologists are neither legal nor financial experts; and that financial planners are not qualified to deal with legal or emotional issues, you can see the benefit of having a team of professionals working on your behalf. Your team will ensure that you walk away from the proceedings in the best possible emotional and financial circumstances within the appropriate legal framework.

The right professional in eight easy steps

To build an effective team, you must choose professionals with whom you can work, and who will be working for your best interests. Here are some tips to help you find professionals who are right for you:

1. Start by getting referrals from family and friends, or other professionals with whom you have worked.

2. Look for professionals with whom you are comfortable. It is important that that person's style matches your needs. Some people in the midst of a divorce want to feel in control, some want to feel empowered, and some simply want direction and a lot of hand-holding. A professional who takes direction from the client but gives little unsolicited input will not suit the latter type of client, but will be raved about by the person who wants control.

3. Ask the professionals you are considering hiring about their experience in dealing with your particular issues. You are within your right to ask for references, and if appropriate, to be shown samples of their work.

4. Check references. It can be very costly changing a professional in mid-stream. Ask the person who referred you what he or she was looking for when he or she hired that professional, and what he or she liked most and least about working with that person. Ask also what the reference would change if he or she were doing it over.

5. Find out what the professional's fee structure is, how you will be billed, and for what you will be billed. Ask for a ballpark figure for the work to be done. But don't make your decision based on price alone. The final price will be determined by many factors outside the professional's — and your — control. Financial advisors must be particularly careful when it comes to method of payment. If they are paid or are going to be paid by commissions from future sales, they may be open to charges of conflict of interest, which will negate the integrity of their opinion if the case does end up in court. It is best for you to ensure that your entire team is paid on a fee-only basis.

6. Ask about service details. How soon can you expect your calls to be returned? What happens to your case if the person with whom you are dealing falls ill or something else comes up?

7. Ask about anything else that is of concern to you.

8. When you are meeting with a professional for the first time, take someone along who knows you and whose opinion you trust. Compare notes afterwards.

During the divorce process, you may also need the services of accountants, appraisers, actuaries, and career counselors for the following reasons:

- *Accountants* can analyze books of a business to determine the value of the business — very useful in cases in which one or the other party has business interests. An accountant can also help you determine whether or not your spouse has hidden assets.

- *Appraisers* can determine the monetary value of any particular asset, thereby giving you much-needed information when you are bargaining a settlement. How much is your house worth? Or your collection of antiques? Or a stamp or coin collection? An appraiser can help you answer all these questions.

- *Actuaries* are people who compile and analyze statistics. Actuaries are normally used to calculate the real value of a pension, which can be difficult to determine. The value of a pension shown on a pension fund's annual report may or may not be useful for property-division purposes. A pension is a valuable asset, and you'll want the most accurate figures possible when working out your divorce settlement.

- *Career counselors* are used whenever information about career possibilities and choices are required. A career counselor may be used to evaluate the potential future earning of a spouse, for the purpose of determining spousal support. For example, suppose one spouse had supported the family while the other went to medical school or law school, and the divorce happened soon after the newly graduated spouse entered the workforce. A career counselor may be consulted to determine the future earning potential of that spouse so that proper restitution can be made.

Another instance in which a career counselor may be used is if one spouse stayed home as a caregiver to the family. During the divorce proceedings, the supporting spouse may make allegations as to the high-earning potential of the stay-at-home spouse due to previous education. A counselor can give a realistic view of the stay-at-home spouse's income potential due to age, education, experience, and workplace demands. A career counselor can also help you move forward into your post-divorce life.

A qualified, well-chosen team working on your behalf can help you avoid mistakes and decisions that could prove very costly to your future. The financial effects of divorce are not only immediate. They can also persist right into old age.

The following article is from the Smart Marriages Archive, reproduced in the *Divorce Statistics Collection* by Eric Beauch-esne, Southam News, Monday, December 20, 1999. The data referred to in this article is Canadian. However, because Canadian and American demographics are so similar, it could just as easily be applied to the United States.

OTTAWA — Baby boomers, particularly women, may end up paying a high price in old age for their soaring divorce rates, a cost that tax payers would likely share.

A collection of essays by Statistics Canada and university researchers on the "consequences of population ageing" warns of the impact for divorced elderly boomers and for their adult children.

"A number of events could interfere with the effectiveness or the informal support network of the elderly in the future, the most significant of which is probably divorce," it says. "A number of surveys tend to show that the helping relationships and exchanges among divorced parents and children are not as strong as others, mainly in the case of men."

However, it is divorced female boomers who are in danger of being the major victims in old age, at least financially, and that could weigh heavily on the cash-starved and strained social safety net.

Divorce may already be hurting elderly parents of divorced baby boomers.

"Divorced parents are inclined to give less, both financially and in terms of other forms of support, to their adult children," said one of the authors, Ingrid Connidis, director of the interdisciplinary group on ageing at the University of Western Ontario in London, Ontario. "In turn, adult children who are divorced are inclined to give less to their parents, and adult children whose parents are divorced are less inclined to give to their divorced parents.

"In general, women suffer more financially than men do," Ms. Connidis said in an interview. "It's a function of divorce, there's no question.

"But if you compare men who have divorced with men who have not divorced, they also experience financial consequences," she said. "They have fewer financial resources than their married male counterparts.

"Overall, however, it tends to be women who suffer more financially as a consequence of divorce," she said.

Widowhood is currently the major reason unattached elderly women, who have among the highest poverty rate of any group of Canadians at 42%, are without a spouse and the financial support that offers.

That is changing. "Trends in divorce rates indicate that widowhood will decline, and divorce will increase as the basis for being unattached in old age," says the report, to be published in print and on the Internet early next year.

"On the one hand, we can assume that the difference in life expectancy between men and women will shrink, with the result that more couples will be together in old and very old age," it notes. "On the other hand, divorce, which is rising sharply in this generation, will deprive a number of baby boomers of a spouse."

The divorce rate among baby boomers is sharply higher than among earlier generations, Statistics Canada census data show.

The proportion of the population that was divorced at age 35 to 44 was about 14% for boomers born between 1947 and 1961, dramatically greater than the 10% for people born between 1937 – 46, 6% for those born from 1927 – 36 and a mere 1% for those born from 1917 – 26.

"If anything, the divorce rates may greatly understate the level of family breakups," says Leroy Stone, Statistics Canada's associate director general of analytical studies.

"It could be that as you go deeper into the baby boom generation, you had more and more people staying out of marriages and going into common law, so that by the time they got to 35 to 44, there'd be less of them to be divorced because they hadn't got married in the first place," he says.

"And the breakups in common law are way, way higher than in legal marriages. I mean way higher, and the impacts on children are really sobering because they tend to happen when the children are really young much more often than with the legal marriages."

That would suggest the bonds between common-law couples and between them and their children would be even weaker after a split than among members of a family divided by divorce.

And on balance, the researchers "predict that the number of individuals living alone in old age will show new and sustained growth" once the first of the baby boomers begins to reach age 65 in 2011.

But divorce, not to mention the breakup of common-law relationships, may not only "lower the amount of support from children to their older parents" but also the financial help that the parents are able or willing to give their adult children.

Research has shown "that older parents with intact marriages give more support for their adult children than do those whose marriages have been disrupted by widowhood or divorce."

"The problem that we have when we talk either about government policy or the implications of trends," said Ms.

Connidis, "is that we apply our current understanding to a very different group of people.

"If we look at the parents of the baby boom, they've generally been fairly well off," she said. "The situation for the baby boom could be quite different."

A problem, however is that researchers don't know what the price to individuals, and taxpayers, of divorce on the elderly might be because most research has focused on the impact on children.

Bob Glossop, of the Vanier Institute of the Family, agrees with the Statistics Canada report that more research is needed.

"We've never thought forward to the impact of divorce on an ageing population," he noted.

And there are potential safety nets for divorced women. For example, more have been in the labor force than in earlier generations, they tend to be closer to their children after a divorce, and they appear more able to form social support networks than men.

The purpose of including the above article is to make the point that financial reality, not emotions, should be a primary motivator in the settlement negotiation process.

Your future — not the playing out of old patterns or the settling of old scores — is what your divorce settlement should be all about. Staying focused on the future can help you obtain the best settlement possible.

Chapter 2

The Language of Separation and Divorce

It is still not enough for language to have clarity and content …
it must also have a goal and an imperative.

— René Daumal (1908 – 1944), French poet

The separation and divorce process is akin to waking up in a foreign country. Lost and confused, you have just enough knowledge of the language to know that you are missing the substance of the conversation. Consider this section your quick-start travel guide. Its purpose is to explain the essential terms of the language of separation and divorce. Understanding the language will help make it easier for you to follow the process you now find yourself facing.

This list is not complete. It is not a list of legal definitions; it is a list of user-friendly definitions, which may mean that it is somewhat generalized. If you want the precise legal definition of any term, it is best to consult a lawyer.

Another caution to keep in mind throughout this book is that nothing in the legal system is written in stone. When a case goes to court, the outcome is dependent on the case itself, the way it is presented, and on the judge who is hearing it. The information presented in this book is intended to help you make informed decisions. It in no way predicts a specific outcome. Always consult the appropriate professional for advice specific to your case.

This information is included as a chapter rather than as a glossary because it is important for you to review the terms before you get into the details.

The following terms will begin your separation and divorce primer:

Access: Visitation rights of the non-custodial parent and other interested parties, such as a grandparent.

Age of majority: The age at which a person acquires all the legal rights of an adult in the jurisdiction in which he or she lives. In most places, this age is assumed to be 18. In some states or provinces, it may be an older age. Check your states or province's Web site for more information on the age of majority in your area.

Annual income: Income earned in one year from all sources, including salary, self-employment, rental, investments, and other sources.

Case law: A term used to reflect how the courts interpret laws. Case law (or common law, as it is sometimes called) is law based on previous decisions by judges.

Child of the marriage: Any dependent child (due to age, disability, or other cause) to whom the married couple acted as parents, including children who are not biologically related to the spouses, such as stepchildren and adopted children.

Community property/marital property/family assets: Property (assets and debts) acquired since the date of the marriage, regardless of the name in which the property is registered. (As property division is governed by state or provincial law, the terms used in the acts vary, but the meaning is usually the same.) The only potential exceptions are inheritances, some insurance settlements, and direct gifts to one party. The word "potential" is important, as different rules apply to different jurisdictions.

Consent order: An agreement between the parties involved in the separation or divorce that has been reviewed by a judge to ensure that it is reasonable. If children are involved, the judge reviews the agreement to ensure that it is in the best interest of the child. Consent orders may be used to change a previous court order.

Contested: A divorce in which there are areas of disagreement; for example, property division, support, or custody.

Court order: The decision or ruling handed down by a judge. For example, when parents cannot agree on child custody or child support, either one may ask the judge to decide.

Court registry: Places where all court records of open cases are kept (usually the courthouse). Your divorce application should be filed at the registry close to your place of residence. There is also a central divorce registry kept by the federal government. If you are not sure if your spouse has filed for divorce, or if you suspect your spouse may have filed for divorce in another state or province, you can check with the central registry.

Divorce: The process laid out by federal law under which a marriage is legally terminated.

Divorce order/decree: The final outcome of divorce proceedings. The order or decree is a court order stating that the marriage is dissolved.

Imputing income: Done when the court feels that the amount of income a spouse claims for the purpose of determining child support payments is too low to be appropriate. In such a case, the court could impute income (i.e., assign an amount) to the spouse whose income is needed to calculate child support. For example, the court may attribute income to a spouse who fails to provide income information requested by the courts, or a spouse who is suddenly unemployed or underemployed for no good reason.

Interim or temporary agreement: An agreement between the two parties on specific issues — such as child support payments or sharing of expenses during separation — which will be effective while the parties work out the rest of the details of the divorce. A lawyer is not required to create an interim or temporary agreement, but it is a good idea to consult with one to ensure that legal rights are not being signed away.

Minor children: Children who have not yet reached the age of majority. If there are minor children involved in a separation, the child's best interest must be the motivating factor in deciding physical custody, access, and guardianship. Parents cannot sign away the rights of a child. Doing so will invalidate any agreement and allow the courts to set up new arrangements.

No-fault divorce: A divorce in which the grounds for divorce are solely that the parties have been living separate and apart for one year.

Pre-divorce syndrome (PDS): A condition suffered by those going through divorce. Symptoms may include feelings of rage, fear, loss, helplessness, pain, misery, hate, anguish, hostility, revenge, loss of self-esteem, and blaming (self or others). Some seek to deal with their feelings using alcohol, drugs, or other destructive behavior. PDS may linger on long after the divorce is finalized.

Separation: The name given to the event that may lead to a divorce. Separation occurs when a married couple has decided that their marriage is no longer working. They have ceased marital relations and are seeking to determine the next step in their relationship. The couple is still legally married during this stage.

Separation agreement: A legally binding contract that details the terms and conditions of the separation as agreed by both parties.

Settlement: The term used to indicate resolution of the financial and other issues upon the dissolution of the marriage.

Uncontested: A divorce in which both parties agree on *all* the issues involved in the divorce.

There are two other terms that deserve further discussion. These are custody and support.

Custody

The term *custody* can be confusing as it can refer to physical custody or legal custody. One must be clear about exactly what is meant by custody.

Physical custody: The disposition of the children of the marriage.

Sole physical custody: A term used to describe an arrangement in which one parent has the children residing with him or her for more than 40 percent of the time. That parent will normally receive child support.

Joint physical custody or shared custody: A term used to describe an arrangement in which both parents have near-equal custody of the children (that is, the children reside approximately half the time with one parent and the other half of the time with the other parent). Both parties are equally responsible for the costs involved in the care and nurturing of the children.

Split custody: Indicates that the children of the marriage are split between the parents. One parent may have sole physical custody of one or more children, while the other parent has sole physical custody of the rest. Child support payments, in these instances, may be very complicated. It is highly advised that you get legal counsel.

Legal custody or guardianship: Terms used to indicate the person who has the right to give legal permission regarding a child's health, education, welfare, and mobility.

Joint guardianship: An arrangement in which both parents are guardians. In such a case, should one parent die, the child will automatically live with the other parent.

Sole guardianship: An arrangement in which only one parent is legally recognized as the guardian of the child. That parent can designate who, upon his or her death, becomes the guardian of the minor child. The parent who has sole guardianship can also make decisions on where to live and what is best for the child without having to obtain the other parent's permission.

Support

There are two distinct types of support: child support and spousal support (also called alimony).

Child support

Even after divorce, both parents have a legal duty to support their children financially. Child support is money paid to the custodial parent for the care and benefit of the children. Every child is entitled to financial support, regardless of whether or not the parents were married.

Both the United States and Canada have laws aimed at protecting the living standards of children involved in separation and divorce.

In the United States, each state is required to have a Child Support Guideline. In some states, it is really only a guideline, and judges have a lot of room to deviate from that guideline. In other states, such as California, judges adhere fairly closely to the guideline. The actual amount of support depends on many factors and the state in which the parties live. For example, some states use net income to calculate the amount of support, while others use gross income. You will have to check with a state agency (see Appendix 3 for Web sites) or see a lawyer to find out the rules in your jurisdiction.

In Canada, the minimum amount payable is based on the Federal Child Support Guidelines. There are individual tables in the guidelines to reflect the different tax rates in each province. Federal tables will apply if no provincial guidelines exist. In Canada, the term "guideline" is somewhat of a misnomer, since it is more mandatory in nature than a guide. Judges may award higher support payments than indicated by the guideline, but only in extreme circumstances will they award less than the guideline amounts. The guideline is based on the payer's income and the number of children involved. This amount is neither taxable to the receiver, nor deductible to the payer if the agreement or court order was made as of May 1, 1997.

If a child has special expenses (i.e., exeptional or extraordinary expenses, over and above child support), these costs are usually shared in proportion to the incomes of the parties involved in the divorce.

Spousal support (alimony)

Spousal support is money paid to relieve any economic inequality that may exist at the end of a marriage. Whether or not a spouse receives support depends on a number of factors; for example —

- need,
- ability of the other spouse to pay,
- length of marriage, and
- age and health.

Either spouse may apply to the courts to vary the amount or terms of spousal support, if his or her personal financial situation changes. Spousal support, when merited, can be time-limited or indefinite; periodic or lump sum.

Time-limited spousal support: Usually granted when the receiving spouse needs financial support while he or she upgrades his or her skills to earn an income, or when the receiving spouse has family obligations that prevent him or her from working full time; for example, while the children are young.

Indefinite spousal support: More likely in a long-term traditional marriage. A traditional marriage is often one in which one spouse gave up his or her career to look after the children and/or to help build the career of the other spouse.

Periodic support: Support paid monthly or annually.

Lump sum: A one-time, non-taxable payment to the receiving spouse, instead of regular, taxable, support payments. A lump-sum payment may sometimes take the form of a higher percentage of the assets to one spouse.

Now that you have a grasp of the language of separation and divorce, as well as a basic grounding in some of the concepts involved, you're ready to proceed to the next chapter for an overview of the separation and divorce process.

From Separation to Divorce: An Overview of the Process

... Immature thinking makes it difficult for them to process the divorce.
They tend to see things in black and white terms
and have trouble putting events into perspective.

— Mary Pipher (20th century),
US clinical psychologist

Even though divorce is common in our society, it is, in general, a poorly understood procedure. Understandably, it seems that many people are truly interested in finding out the requirements and details of the process only if they themselves or a close friend or relative is involved. It is important, though, to understand the divorce process thoroughly and to recognize all the options you have available to you *before* you make any decisions concerning your future. It is during this process that you will be negotiating finances, the division of property, and possibly even support for yourself and your children. It is important that knowledge — rather than your emotions or other people's opinions — guide you. Informed decisions, rather than emotional ones, are more likely to produce the long-term results most beneficial to you. Surprisingly enough, knowledge also helps to calm the emotions, since it reduces fear of the unknown.

All divorces start with a separation and end with a divorce decree. It is what happens between these two points that makes the difference in the financial and emotional cost of the divorce process.

This chapter examines separation, the elements of the divorce process, and then moves to a brief description of the steps involved in the process itself.

Separation

A separation is a cooling-off period. It is meant to give the couple involved the opportunity — as well as the time and space — to try to work out the problems of their marriage if they can, and should they wish to do so. Since no-fault divorce was introduced, once a couple has been separated for one year, the divorce may proceed, even if it is the wish of only one of the parties. However, the ease of the process, as well as the cost of the divorce, will depend on the other party. If your spouse refuses to cooperate, you may find yourself facing increased legal costs or having your assets tied up for a long period of time. The following example illustrates how this situation can happen:

Hillary and Bill separated because Bill thought Hillary had been unfaithful to him. He wanted to punish her. While he could not stop the divorce from becoming final, he could and did hold up the division of property. He played games, such as refusing to engage a lawyer, so that Hillary's lawyer had to deal with him personally. He ignored requests for information and made unreasonable demands to which he knew she could not agree, all the while causing her to rack up legal bills with her lawyer. When the matrimonial home was sold, the money was withheld from both parties until a settlement was achieved. Hillary could not purchase a new home or move forward with her life. It took over four years and a court trial to get a final property settlement with Bill.

Separation may be delineated in several ways. For example, actual separation may have started between a couple when they ceased having marital relations. Therefore, two people sleeping in the same bed may still be considered separated. It may also have started when one partner moved to another bedroom or into the basement. Therefore, it is quite possible for two people to be separated while still living under the same roof. The most common date of separation used, however, is the date on which one party moves out of the marital home or a date upon which both parties agree.

You should be aware that the date of separation could be very significant, as it may have some bearing on your settlement. This date may be used in determining the value of assets, in determining if a particular debt can be considered a family debt, and in determining exactly when you and your spouse may apply for the divorce decree under the no-fault clause. Consider the following example:

Charles and Diane had agreed that Charles would move out of the matrimonial home January 31, 2002. Unfortunately, he could not move into his new home until February 28, but they remained in separate bedrooms until then. Charles made a contribution to a completely new retirement account on February 13 of that year.

Would that contribution be considered part of the family assets eligible for division? The answer is maybe, and maybe not. If Charles and Diane had agreed, preferably in writing, that the date Charles intended to move out was also the official separation date, then this money may not be a family asset, as it was accumulated after the official separation date and only from Charles's income. If they had no agreement, and Diane contended that the date of separation was actually the date Charles moved out (February 28), that contribution likely would be considered family property.

This date is even more important when a business is involved. Sometimes, if a business is expecting a large order or some other event that will increase its value, the owner going through the divorce may seek to set the date of separation before the triggering event. This strategy could cause significant losses to the other spouse in terms of the business's value. In one such case, a businessman valued his business at eight million dollars. To facilitate a quick separation agreement, he generously offered his spouse four million dollars, plus alimony of $100,000 per year for ten years. She agreed, and the agreement was signed. One year later, he sold the business for forty million dollars. He contended that changes he made to the business in that year dramatically increased its value. Since she could not prove that the business had had a higher value at the time she signed the separation agreement, she was not entitled to the increase in value at the time of the sale.

The same principle would apply to debts, but in reverse. Two people may be physically separated but have no agreement in place nor have bothered to cancel joint credit cards or lines of credit. They have simply assumed that if they are no longer living together, they are no longer responsible for each other's debts. Wrong! Any debts accumulated during the marriage are the responsibility of both parties. This responsibility would normally be shed only if there is an agreed-on separation date and prudent steps are taken to sever joint financial ties, or alternately, on the date the divorce decree is granted.

When agreeing to a date of separation, the parties involved cannot lie as to the actual date simply to facilitate a quick divorce. Lying about the date is considered collusion, which is against the law. If collusion can be proved, the judge in the case may refuse to grant a divorce.

Some people, once separated, never proceed to divorce at all. Whatever their reasons, these couples prefer the married-but-separated state, and sometimes this state has unforeseen advantages. One woman, after a 10-year separation from her husband, became a widow. She applied for — and received — survivor benefits for herself and their children from the social security program since she was still legally his wife and neither of them was in another relationship. However, had her husband been in a common-law relationship for more than one year, that may have impacted her rights. You should be mindful of time limitations and always consult a lawyer in your jurisdiction.

After the separation agreement is in place, some people will proceed with the divorce application only when they reach the point of wanting to remarry. A divorce is necessary to terminate the current marriage. If someone who is only separated remarries without first obtaining a divorce decree, that person would be committing bigamy. Bigamy is against the law — and would render the subsequent marriage invalid.

If you are contemplating separation, see "Tips on Preparing for Separation" in Appendix 2.

The Anatomy of the Divorce Process

The divorce process can be broken down into three elements, which, taken altogether, make up the whole. These elements are not necessarily sequential and may, in fact, proceed simultaneously. When people speak of "getting a divorce," they are usually referring to all the various steps one must take to get to a divorce decree; which can be very confusing, as you will see below.

In reality, the first element, usually called the "divorce," is the actual dissolution of the marriage. It involves applying to the courts to grant a divorce. In the United States, each state has its own divorce laws that govern this process. It is interesting to note that the tax aspects of divorce are overseen by the IRS, which is a federal body. In Canada, divorce is governed by the Divorce Act, which is federal legislation. Regardless of where you live in North America, the end result of "divorce," as meant in this context, is a decree or court order that declares the marriage legally over.

The second element of what people commonly refer to as a divorce is property division; that is, the division of assets and liabilities accumulated during the marriage. The end result of property division is a property settlement. Of course, a property settlement becomes part of the divorce process only if there actually are family assets or debts to be divided. In both the United States and Canada, division of property is governed by state and provincial statutes.

The third element of the divorce process is corollary relief: child and spousal support, and custody and access arrangements. Child and/or spousal support is intended to provide economic relief, and to deal with any inequalities that may exist between the partners, as a result of the marriage. The end result of corollary relief is a support settlement. Corollary relief factors into the divorce process only if there are minor children of the marriage or there is a case for spousal support. Corollary relief is addressed in the laws of each state of the United States. It is also addressed in the Divorce Act in Canada, but may be subject to provincial statutes.

If there are no children or property involved, getting a divorce could simply mean obtaining a decree in the appropriate manner.

Figure 1 illustrates the divorce process.

Figure 1
THE DIVORCE PROCESS

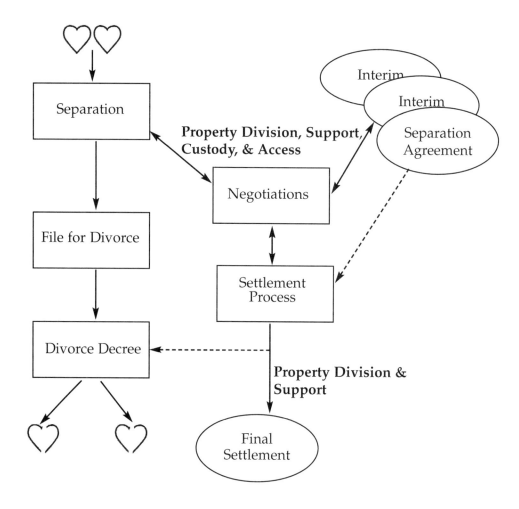

Notice that the divorce process may take several turns. At its simplest, divorce may proceed from separation to filing the paperwork to obtaining the decree, with no other requirements, after which the two individuals proceed as single persons, with no further ties whatsoever. A more common situation, however, is one in which in addition to the filing, the couple negotiate a separation agreement (after a few interim agreements), and they emerge as single persons, but with children and the terms of the separation agreement between them. Then there are always the complicated cases in which settlement negotiations involving property and support may result in several interim agreements being created as the couple gradually resolve their financial affairs, before they emerge as separate individuals again.

When most people think of the divorce process, they automatically think of the traditional or adversarial path to getting a divorce. Today, in addition to the traditional divorce, there are collaborative divorces, mediated divorces, arbitrated divorces, and do-it-yourself divorces. Chapter 4 explores the advantages and disadvantages of each method of divorce and examines under what circumstances each might be appropriate.

Once you have decided upon separation and which path to divorce you wish to take, you must file your paperwork with the courts for your divorce application. You should also start working on settlement negotiations so that you can get your settlement and decree in a timely manner.

Filing for Divorce

Once a spouse has decided to go ahead with the divorce proceeding, the appropriate paperwork needs to be filed with the court registry. Note, however, the divorce will not be granted until the waiting period is over. Who files the paperwork with the courts will depend on which path to divorce you have selected. The laws of the jurisdiction specify which forms are required and the format they must take.

For your personal benefit, it is best if you list both the family assets (everything owned), and liabilities (everything owed) as at the date of separation. It is always interesting to see the values placed on the same assets by each party of the marriage. At this point, getting a complete list is more important than the values assigned. Values can always be verified and assigned later. You may want to use the worksheet provided later in this book to jog your memory and to start your data gathering. If it applies, you should also document what each of you brought into the marriage, both assets and liabilities. The information gathered during this stage will be instrumental in deciding if a property settlement is an issue, and it will give you the information that may be required as part of the filing.

You will need a breakdown of your living expenses. Many jurisdictions ask for living expense information as part of the filing documents, especially if you are requesting support. This is the same information that is in your cash-flow statement. (See Chapter 5 for information on estimating your post-divorce expenses and how to compile a cash-flow statement.)

Keep in mind that to many people, actually filing for a divorce is a very final gesture. It means giving up any hope for this relationship. Any emotional equilibrium that may have been achieved during the separation can now be disrupted again. This is especially true if the reason for the filing is because one partner wants to remarry.

Settlement Negotiations

Ideally, you should start negotiations as soon as you can after you decide to separate so that you can get a separation agreement in place detailing the arrangements between you and your spouse. A separation agreement, however, should not be confused with a divorce settlement. A divorce settlement may include items from the separation agreement but include other agreements as well (see *Settlement* below).

Negotiations may include everything from the division of property to children's issues (support, custody, and access), to spousal support, to custody of the family pet, and visitation rights of in-laws.

For your negotiations to be successful, you must be prepared for a lot of interaction with your spouse, a great deal of discussion, and a fair amount of give and take. Most often, it is during the separation and negotiation stage that emotions are acted out. Some people act out of hurt, guilt, pride, or simply the desire to punish the other spouse. But emotional reactions can be very costly.

Many women involved in a divorce simply want out of the relationship and therefore do not take the time or care to negotiate the best settlement for themselves. A woman may also want to prove that she doesn't need her former spouse, and as a result, will reject the financial assets to which she may be entitled. Usually within four to five years, she realizes her mistake, but by then it is too late.

Notwithstanding the above, however, it is a fallacy that only women are prone to emotionally motivated financial mismanagement during a divorce. That is not true. Some men, especially if they have left their spouses because of other women, will, out of guilt, try to overcompensate. They, too, may find themselves in financial difficulty following their divorces.

The best way to decide if a settlement is appropriate is to have it modeled by a qualified financial planner or a certified divorce specialist and obtain independent legal advice. The financial specialist will be able to show the long-term effects of the settlement on both parties. Having the numbers laid out before you can help you separate the emotions caused by your split with your spouse from the actual financial reality you may be facing post-divorce. Chapter 5 examines money issues in more detail, and provides information to help you determine how much money you will need post-divorce, as well as which assets may or may not be worth your while to keep.

Depending on the method of divorce you choose to use, settlement negotiations may involve temporary (or interim) agreements and a process called discovery.

Discovery is the procedure in which the lawyer for one party questions the other party involved in the divorce. The purpose of discovery is to verify facts and look for new information that may have bearing on the divorce settlement.

Settlement

A settlement is the final agreement on all the issues involved in the divorce. The settlement is usually based on the separation agreement, if there is one. Sometimes, the separation agreement is all that is used. If both parties are happy with the separation agreement, then the terms and conditions contained within it are implemented as is, and no other formal settlement agreement is required.

If you and your spouse have any contested issues between you, then you have two choices. You can either reach a settlement between yourselves or have one imposed on you by the courts, by the way of a trial.

A settlement that you and your spouse reach between yourselves is called an out-of-court settlement. The majority of contested divorces (about 90 percent) are, in fact, settled out of court. A couple may be set to go to court, but as the pressure, the cost, and the nearness of the court date grow, so does the inclination to settle. Sometimes contested-divorce settlements are reached "on the court steps," simply to avoid the trial. Keep in mind that the outcome of a trial cannot be predicted. The way a judge sees the facts may be very different from the way you and your lawyer see them.

Out-of-court settlements are, by far, the better alternative, since they are much less expensive. In the United States, the legal bill for a three-day divorce trial can commonly reach US$70,000 to US$100,000. In Canada, a trial of the same length will cost each individual about CDN$50,000.

Divorce Decree

The divorce decree is obtained by making an application to the courts to grant the divorce order or decree. This application is usually made after all other paperwork has been filed and approved by the court. The order is the piece of paper that makes each party single again and allows each to legally remarry, should they wish to do so.

If you and your spouse have reached a final settlement of corollary relief and property division, it can become part of your divorce order. If the settlement is not completed at the time the divorce order is granted, it may be dealt with as a separate order.

The essential components of a divorce may be the same for everyone, but there are several divorce models now in use. Choosing the one that is right for you can keep your path to your divorce decree from being more difficult than it needs to be. Chapter 4 is an examination of each model.

Divorce: The Five Models, Their Advantages, and Their Consequences

To have his path made clear for him is the aspiration of every human being in our beclouded and tempestuous existence.

— Joseph Conrad (1857 – 1924),
Polish-born British novelist

Today, a couple can choose from among many ways for getting from separation to the divorce decree. Traditional, mediated, arbitrated, collaborative, and do-it-yourself models are all viable means of obtaining a settlement and divorce decree. You can even have a "designer" divorce that you create by selecting and using parts of the different processes to meet your own particular needs. This chapter gives a brief description of the different divorce models currently in use and the situations suited to each.

Traditional Divorce

As mentioned before, the traditional model of divorce is an adversarial process. I feel it is more effective in situations in which there exists a huge imbalance of power, and one party cannot deal with the other in any meaningful way. Sometimes, in cases of physical, mental, or sexual abuse, traditional divorce is the only type that may work.

The first step in a traditional divorce is that one or the other person involved goes out and hires a lawyer. Many people view this action as a declaration of war.

The lawyer files the divorce paperwork, the other party is served, and the formalities begin. The responding party may choose to get a lawyer or may attempt to represent himself or herself. Those who choose to represent themselves often eventually end up getting a lawyer.

Traditional divorce can become an arena in which the parties battle for compensation for hurts or, in some cases, revenge. It is frequently viewed that the person with the better or more aggressive lawyer "wins."

Once engaged, the lawyers become the gateway for communication. The lawyers communicate with each other, then each lawyer will communicate the result of that interaction to his or her client. Each lawyer then gets his or her client's input, combines that input with his or her knowledge and experience, and fires off another round of communication to the other party's lawyer.

As the majority of negotiations are done through the lawyers, it isn't hard to understand how the parties may become even more alienated from each other than they were to begin with, which in turn causes hardening of their respective positions. This cycle repeats itself until there is either an agreement (which may or may not be satisfactory to both parties) or the couple ends up in court for a trial — where the judge makes the decisions, based, of course, on the facts of the case.

Sometimes people involved in a traditional divorce to change lawyers two or possibly more times by the end of the process. Changing lawyers is a costly move, as the client will have to pay each lawyer to come up to speed on the case. Usually, a person changes lawyers because he or she did not understand how to go about hiring the right professional for his or her own needs in the first place. Many clients are looking for support and direction that is not the lawyer's to give. Lawyers are trained to deal with the legal issues of a case, not the emotional or financial aspects.

The product of the traditional model of divorce is, in many cases, bitterness and settlements with which neither party is truly happy. Consider that the traditional model for divorce has the reputation of being a win/lose scenario. Most participants go into the process with (in many cases, unrealistically) high expectations, based on lack of knowledge or faulty logic. They see themselves as entitled to compensation for hurt or suffering — or sometimes simply expect fairness from the system. If the final settlement is a result of a court-imposed decision, the judge's decision is based on the law and what he or she considers fair to both parties. If the final settlement is an out-of-court one, it means that in order to reach the settlement, both sides had to compromise. In either case, both parties seem to focus on what they did *not* get when measured against their original expectations. In their minds, each came out the loser, hence the bitterness and unhappiness.

This process can become very nasty and very, very costly.

Mediated Divorce

In the interests of reducing costs and having a more amicable divorce, the mediation process was born.

The mediated divorce most often involves one mediator who, as a neutral third party, acts to help both members of the couple resolve the matters in dispute between them. The goal of mediation is to help the couple draft the outline of an agreement settling the issues between them, such as finance, child custody, and property division.

A mediator may be anyone who has mediation training and is knowledgeable about the issues involved in a divorce. Mediators may be lawyers, psychologists, social workers, or financial planners. Do be careful when selecting a mediator. Anyone can call himself or herself a mediator. Check his or her training and experience, and see if he or she belongs to a professional organization.

If you and your spouse choose to have a mediated divorce, you should be aware that the mediator cannot wear two hats at the same time. For example, if you engage a lawyer to be the mediator, that person cannot give legal advice in the mediation process. If you hire a financial planner, he or she cannot give financial advice during the mediation process. Because the mediator acts as a neutral third party, he or she can provide only information. There is a fine line between information and advice. Information means giving facts; advice means giving strategy and professional opinions. Providing advice is out-of-bounds during mediation.

Once the couple, with the help of the mediator, has managed to draft an outline of their terms, they will need a lawyer to take the outline and prepare a formal separation or settlement agreement. Before signing the settlement, each party should have his or her own lawyer independently advise him or her on the pros and cons of the terms of the settlement. You do not want, unknowingly, to sign away any legal rights you may have. The advice of a lawyer who has remained outside the mediation process and who is not advising or involved with your spouse in any way can help you ensure that your rights are protected.

Once the couple has their separation agreement in place, the next step is for them to decide if they want to file for divorce now or later. Whoever is most anxious to dissolve the marriage will usually start the proceeding. They may choose to file the paperwork themselves, get a lawyer to do the work, or get one of the companies that specialize in filing divorce paperwork to do it for them.

Mediated divorce, while it can be quick and relatively inexpensive, can be very demanding of the parties involved. It requires a commitment to acting with clearheaded maturity during a very trying time.

Mediation works best when both members of the couple truly want the divorce. They must also both want to use mediation. If one party is reluctant to do so, mediation can become a costly endeavor, as the participants are not obligated to agree to the outline at the end of the process. In this situation, the couple will have wasted the money spent on mediation, and they will have to start again using some other model of divorce.

The couple should also be able to communicate with each other. Each should have a sense of what he or she needs from the process, should be assertive, and must be willing to compromise. Both should both have a good understanding of their finances and the consequences of making certain financial decisions — or alternatively, be willing to get expert help to make them aware of what they may be doing.

Mediation may not work very well if one spouse is feeling strong emotions, such as hurt, anger, resentment, or distrust. It will not work if both are not fully committed to a non-confrontational settlement that is acceptable to both of them.

Settlements resulting from the mediation model are usually quite satisfactory to both parties. Even if both parties have compromised to reach the settlement, they understand the payoff for each compromise. However, I cannot stress enough that the success of mediation and therefore the quality of the settlement is highly dependent on the maturity of the participants and the competence of the mediator.

Arbitrated Divorce

When a couple find themselves very far apart in their positions but nonetheless do not want to go to court, they may opt for an arbitrated divorce. By using arbitration, the couple is allowing someone else to decide on a settlement for them, after hearing the facts of the case. The arbitrator is usually a retired judge or a lawyer, and may be used for the entire process or only to settle individual issues, such as child custody, support, or property division.

When engaging the arbitrator, the couple can choose whether the decision by the arbitrator will be binding or advisory. In binding arbitration, the decision of the arbitrator is binding on both parties — meaning both must accept it — and it becomes a court order, just as it would if a judge had made the ruling. In advisory arbitration, the parties can take the decision under consideration, but are not bound by it.

In addition to being used in the circumstances described above, arbitration is also used in jurisdictions where the courts have a backlog of divorce cases and the parties want a timely decree.

In a surprising number of cases, being heard is as important as the settlement. The spouse who sees himself or herself as being wronged needs to vent anger and frustration, especially to someone whom he or she sees as an impartial party with the power to possibly punish. These people will pursue their need to be heard at the expense of their financial well-being. One such woman spent more then one hundred thousand dollars on legal fees, just to get her day in court. She was able to accept the divorce after that and get on with her life. One man, to be able to tell his story in court, spent his portion of the matrimonial home (his only asset) on legal fees. For such people, the arbitrated divorce works well. Since they are prepared to go to court for a decision, they are usually willing to accept the decision of an arbitrator, warts and all. The difference is that the cost is a lot less than a full-fledged court trial.

The couple using an arbitrator to get a settlement may have already had their marriage dissolved and are now dealing with the "sticky" issues. If they are still married, they have the same options as the couple using a mediator when it comes to filing the paperwork to dissolve their marriage.

Canadian readers may wish to note that arbitration is not often used in Canada for family law disputes.

Collaborative Divorce

The collaborative divorce is the newest innovation in obtaining a divorce. It is meant to be a supportive process designed to help both parties. The most innovative part of the process is that both parties and their lawyers are committed, in writing, to reaching a negotiated agreement out of court. The ultimate goal is to arrive at a solution with which both members of the couple can live.

It is also a team approach to divorce. Each party involved in a collaborative divorce has his or her own lawyer to advise him or her. The lawyers form the core of the team; however, when necessary, other professionals (such as counselors [also called divorce coaches], financial planners specializing in divorce, business valuators, child psychologists, career counselors, or any other resource person that the couple involved might need) are called in to help.

Collaborative divorce uses the four-way process, a technique in which both parties and their lawyers or divorce coaches get together to work on divorce issues. The couple is shown realistic choices regarding their settlement and the consequences of those choices. Co-operation, not conflict, is the key. Collaborative divorce is more effective for couples who want to be in charge and responsible for the results of the divorce.

A collaborative divorce starts with both parties and their lawyers meeting to go over and sign a contract setting out the terms and conditions of the process. The contract addresses the openness and honesty of all parties concerned. It addresses as well the role of the lawyers as legal advisors and their commitment to an out-of-court solution.

Really, the lawyers are there to give legal advice and to let the clients know when their expectations are unreasonable, to manage emotions, and to get other qualified professionals to advise both members of the couple when they require certain information to make prudent decisions.

The next step in the process is for both parties to state their needs, wants, and expectations. Information is gathered on the resources available to the couple. Areas of conflict or potential conflict are noted, and a plan to handle those areas is established.

The parties then enter into negotiation on the basis of what is best for all concerned. Counselors are used to help "clear the air" emotionally, if needed. Their central role is in helping with post-divorce communication and assisting with parenting issues. If the couple require it, counselors are available to facilitate a healing process. Other professionals may be called in during the negotiation to provide relevant information.

Once a settlement is reached, both lawyers will help the couple get the necessary court approvals.

If, for whatever reason, the couple cannot come to a settlement and have to go to court, their collaborative lawyers must step aside. These lawyers cannot represent either party in court.

On hearing of the team approach, people automatically think this model must be an expensive alternative to the others. This assumption is not necessarily correct. To date, the cost of a collaborative divorce is averaging less than that of a traditional divorce and produces a better settlement.

There are two things that rack up costs in a traditional divorce: uneducated proposals and duplication of effort. Clients and their lawyers draw up proposals focused on the needs of only one party. The communication pattern is back-and-forth between the lawyer/client/lawyer in an effort to come up with an acceptable solution. If one party engages a professional to provide an informed opinion on some matter, the other party may want to hire his or her own professional to verify or refute the information. There are also costs involved in document preparation and retaining expert witnesses, as well as general court costs. The whole process can be very time consuming and costly.

In the collaborative approach, any professionals used are neutral. Therefore, only one fee — rather than two — is paid to get information both parties can use. Since the settlement is hammered out by both members of the couple together based on the same information and choices, both parties have an understanding of why certain terms that may not be ideal are nonetheless for the best. The cost of a collaborative divorce, in the long run, may be the most inexpensive, both financially and emotionally, for contested divorces.

Do-It-Yourself Divorce

In legal circles, this kind of divorce is called a desk-order divorce.

A person does not necessarily need a lawyer to get a divorce. In fact, a recent study suggests that 78 percent of those going through a divorce are unrepresented.

If both parties want the divorce, if there are no children involved, if there are no spousal support issues, and if both agree on the division of any property, the do-it-yourself divorce may be a viable option.

Those who have the time and like to follow a defined process are the ones best suited for this model. The most daunting prospect of this whole process is filling out the forms required and filing them. There are many books written for those who choose this option. Self-Counsel Press's *Divorce Guides* are designed to help people complete their own divorces by showing them how to fill out the forms required and telling them what to do at each stage.

A do-it-yourself divorce can save you a great deal in legal fees, as no lawyer is required.

However, even for this option, I would suggest that you and your spouse create a separation agreement and that you each have independent lawyers review the agreement before you sign it.

Considerations for Selecting a Divorce Model

For many, the major considerations to selecting a divorce model are cost and time. It is estimated that the average traditional divorce — if there is no trial involved — costs about $5,000 to

$15,000 per person, and takes between 18 months and up to 3 years to complete. A mediated divorce averages from $2,500 and $5,000 for the couple, and could take about one year to complete. A collaborative divorce averages from $2,500 to $5,000 per person, plus out-of-pocket expenses. It takes 6 to 18 months to complete. A do-it-yourself divorce can cost less than $2,000 for both parties. The amount of time it takes depends on who is doing the paperwork and filing.

However, when selecting a divorce model, another factor should be added to this mix: the type of separation the couple experienced. The reason for the separation is a major emotional element that must be taken into consideration. The type of separation you have experienced may indicate which divorce model is most appropriate for you.

The most important outcome of your divorce process is the settlement, and the settlement starts with the separation agreement. Therefore, the dynamics involved in obtaining the separation agreement are crucially important.

Abuse-motivated separation

The hardest type of separation to handle is one that has been motivated by abuse. Whether the abuse is mental or physical, the power imbalance between the members of the couple is obvious. It takes a lot of courage for the abused spouse to leave.

Unfortunately, that same imbalance is almost sure to come into play in the creation of the separation agreement. One spouse may still try to exert control over the other. This situation is poorly suited to either a do-it-yourself or a mediated solution.

Depending on the extent of the need of one party to control the other, even a collaborative solution may be difficult. Sad as it may be, abused spouses, even though they have managed to leave the relationship, are still at risk emotionally, physically, and financially. They need to put as much distance between themselves and their ex-partners as possible. The traditional divorce may help them to keep that distance.

Trial separation

When one or both members of a couple wish to save the marriage, they may opt for a trial separation. The point of such a separation is to give the couple the time and space to see if they are happier apart than they were together.

A trial separation is usually an attempt to change some behavior in the marriage. Because one or both people involved are hoping to get back together, they do not see the need for a separation agreement.

Yet an agreement can be very beneficial to couples in this situation. In addition to spelling out the sharing of expenses and the particulars of child custody and visitation, the agreement can also encompass such things as counseling. These couples can use the creation of the agreement as a vehicle to express not only their expectations, but also what each needs for this marriage to work.

The collaborative process will work very well with this couple. The use of divorce coaches will be helpful in bringing needs and expectations to the surface. The co-coaching approach may work a great deal better than the traditional marriage counseling, since both parties are able to work on their own issues as well as their issues as a couple.

Forced separation

A forced separation occurs when one spouse simply leaves the other. The "left" spouse is taken by surprise because he or she may have been perfectly content with the way things were. In this situation, the two spouses are poles apart along the divorce route. One has been thinking of it for a while and has weighed his or her options, come to terms with separation and prepared for it, and is ready to deal with it.

The other spouse is feeling shell-shocked. He or she cannot understand what has happened, or why. Most likely, that person will want to try to make the marriage work and cannot comprehend that the other party may already be involved with someone else. For the leaving spouse, however, the marriage had been over for a long time; it's just that he or she did not — up to now— have a concrete reason to leave. Sometimes, this reason comes in the form of an outside love interest; sometimes, it is the death of a parent or friend; and sometimes, it is just the realization of how unhappy he or she has been in the marriage.

This couple has most likely stopped communicating a long time ago, and a separation will not repair that rift. Often, both parties feel a great deal of anger and resentment. How these powerful emotions will play out depends on the characters of the individuals involved. For reasons of pride or guilt, one spouse may want very little out of the marriage. Alternatively, the other spouse may want more than his or her entitlement as a form of revenge or punishment.

The collaborative divorce may also work very well following this type of separation. Through the collaborative model, the couple may be able to work through their feelings, get the children any help needed, and get the financial help they will need to sort out their financial affairs. As a result, they may find their way to a much better settlement than could be obtained through the other models.

Mutually agreed separation

Sometimes, both parties have agreed to end the marriage. They may want to do so amicably, with as little cost as possible. Both feel that they are reasonable, fair people and that they should have no problem coming to a resolution. This situation is often called a mutually agreed separation.

In such a scenario, the couple would draw up the separation agreement, have it looked over by an inexpensive lawyer, then file the paperwork for the divorce. If all goes well, they may even remain friends after the divorce. While this is the best of all worlds, there may still be pitfalls. Look at Jenny and Sam's story:

Jenny and Sam had been married 32 years. Their children were grown and had started families of their own. Jenny and Sam had grown apart over the years and no longer had the same interests or goals.

After a lot of civilized conversation, they decided to part company. Sam was an executive at a large company, and made an excellent salary. Jenny had kept up a part-time career during the years the kids were growing up.

Their agreement stipulated that Sam would pay Jenny spousal support until he retired, which he had planned would be at age 65.

Jenny geared her life and lifestyle to that agreement. She purchased a home and car in such a manner that her payments for these things would end when Sam turned 65.

At the time of their separation, they were both content with this agreement.

Five years later, when Sam was 62, his company went through a major downsize. Sam was given a very generous severance package.

Sam immediately stopped making support payments to Jenny. He contended that he was now retired and was no longer required to make the payments. Jenny contended that they had agreed that the payments would continue until Sam reached age 65.

They have been fighting over this issue now for two years. Jenny is running into debt because of the unexpected drop in her income. Sam has had his assets frozen.

After a costly battle, Jenny got her back support and her agreement was upheld.

It is easy to see that if you select the wrong model of divorce, your settlement can be significantly affected.

Consider what may happen if a couple who separated because of abuse chose the mediation process because of cost. If the process worked at all, the person with the stronger personality would likely end up with the settlement he or she wanted, while the more passive partner would suffer financial deprivation. You must carefully consider not only all the elements you want included in your settlement, but also the path you want to take to that settlement.

Now that you've reviewed the divorce process, familiarized yourself with the language of divorce, and reviewed the various models available to you, you need to move on to determining what sort of financial condition you want to find yourself in following your divorce. The next chapter deals with the all-important nuts and bolts of your money issues.

Chapter 5

Your Money Issues

Money is the sinews of love, as of war.
— George Farquhar (1678 – 1707), Irish dramatist

The majority of those going through a divorce have one big, looming question: "How will I fare, financially, after this divorce is complete?" The time to begin thinking about your money issues, however, is not while you are in the middle of your divorce, and certainly not once the divorce has happened. You'll be in a much stronger position if you start to address your money issues at the point at which you find yourself considering separation or divorce. You'll not only feel better, but you'll be better off for having worked through these issues sooner rather than later.

From a financial planning point of view, there are many areas that you must consider during the separation and divorce process. Some will affect your separation agreement, while others will affect your lifestyle. This chapter attempts to address these issues in order of importance.

However, to address the money issues effectively, you will have to do some preparatory work. You will have to determine the resources that will be available to you. The output from this exercise will be two documents, both of which you will find useful in the separation and divorce process no matter which model of divorce you choose. They are the net worth statement and the cash flow statement.

If you have not been keeping records of your income and expenses, you will have to do some extra work gathering this information. If you are a record keeper, you probably already have most of the information you require for this exercise.

Get a binder, a basket, a file folder, or something to keep all the information you collect in one place. Next, obtain the most recent pay stubs available for both you and your spouse. Obtain all the financial statements (bank, charge cards, mortgage, pensions, investments, registered investments, savings accounts, etc.) you can find. To be thorough, you want all joint statements, plus anything that is in your name or your spouse's name alone. Remember, marital assets are assets accumulated during the marriage, regardless of who actually owns the asset.

Net Worth Statement

First, you are going to work on your net worth statement. This statement is a snapshot of every financial decision you have made to date. It shows you the results of those decisions by summarizing your financial life as it is at this moment. It is a record of everything you own (assets) and everything that you owe (liabilities).

At the back of this book in Appendix 1, you will find a number of worksheets to help you organize your finances. Use Worksheet 1 to help you determine your net worth as a couple. While filling in Worksheet 1 keep the following in mind:

- For items that may have tax consequences, fill in the original value of the item whenever possible. This would include real estate, other than your personal residence, non-registered mutual funds, shares in a business, art, antiques, and collectibles. (For your convenience, these items are marked by an asterisk on the worksheet.) What you are looking for, if you have it, is the cost of the asset when you bought it plus the cost of any renovations; or in the case of investments, re-invested dividends. This is also known as an adjusted cost base and is used to calculate income tax liability on all non-registered investment assets, including the family cottage or vacation property. You will notice on the liability portion of the net worth worksheet that there are items that are also marked by an asterisk, such as investment and margin loans. The original amount is *not* required here, but it is useful to have for your information as it can show where some of your money went.

- If the asset is held in the husband's name, put the value of the asset in the "His" column. If it is held in the wife's name, put the value in the "Her" column. As stated before, any asset acquired during the marriage is still part of the matrimonial property to be divided between the parties regardless of in whose name it is held. This method of recording assets makes it easier to track the assets by noting who has possession of what at the time of separation. Also, when it comes time to divide the assets, instead of going through the complexity of dividing everything, it may be easier to divide the assets by allocating what is in one person's name to that person first, then arranging for the transfer of assets from the other party to fulfill the separation agreement.

    Put any items registered in joint names into the "Joint" column.

- Please note that any growth in a registered education savings plan or any money invested "in trust" for the children does not belong to the parents. Therefore, do not include these amounts in your net worth statement.

- The net worth statement is a summary. The rows that apply to you are to be filled in with the sum total of individual assets or debts. For example, if you have two rental properties in joint names for which the market value is $200,000 each, you will fill in $400,000 in the "Joint" column of the real estate row under investments. If those properties were purchased for $125,000 each, then $250,000 will be entered in the "Original Value" column.

If you do not have the information for some asset or liability, don't panic. At least now you know what you don't know and can find some way to get this information. It would also be helpful to keep track of the details of each category as you go along. For example, you would record separately that the real estate category is made up of two properties, the address of each, the original cost, the dates purchased, mortgages against each, and any other information that you think might be important. If you have investment accounts at several institutions, you may want to write down the account numbers, the institution, the amount in that account, and the type of account, such as retirement. Sample 1 illustrates how the Net Worth Worksheet might look once it is completed.

Your assets, or what you own

The following contains brief descriptions of each of the asset categories show on the net worth worksheet:

Bank accounts: Include both checking and saving accounts.

Savings: Include guaranteed investment certificates (GICs), term deposits, short-term government bonds, or any other short-term savings held outside a savings account.

Life insurance cash value: Indicate the amount that the policy will pay out now if you cashed it in, not the amount it will pay out on death. There is normally no cash value in term policies.

Residence: Indicate the realistic current market value of the matrimonial home. If you have no idea what this might be, call an appraiser or realtor and ask for how much similar homes have been selling in your neighborhood.

Recreational property: Indicate the current market value of your cottage or time-share condo in Arizona. This category includes any property the family uses for recreational purpose only.

Collectibles/valuables: Indicate the value of motor homes, boats, motorcycles, tools, car collections, antiques, stamp collections, or anything else of value. Again, if you have no idea, you may wish to call in an appraiser who specializes in that particular area.

Vehicles: Indicate the value of your personal vehicles. The best value to show is not what it is worth to you, but what a dealer would pay for it should you sell it.

Sample 1
NET WORTH

Assets	Original Value*	Ownership — Joint	Ownership — His	Ownership — Hers	Household Totals
Personal					
Bank accounts		$2,000			
Savings		$5,000	$1,000	$1,500	
Life insurance cash value (not death benefit)			$4,500		
Residence		$450,000			
Recreational property*	$80,000	$140,000			
Collectibles/valuables*					
Vehicles			$35,000	$11,000	
Furniture		$16,000			
Investments					
Pension plans			$214,000	$82,000	
Company savings plan			$17,000		
Registered investments				$76,000	
Non-registered investments*	$100,000	$120,000			
Non-registered stocks*					
Offshore investments					
Real estate*	$250,000	$400,000			
Business*					
Trust fund					
Other investments					
Total (A)		$1,133,000	$271,500	$170,500	$1,575,000
Liabilities					
Credit cards		$3,200		$1,600	
Taxes owed			$1,200		
Lines of credit		$7,000			
Retirement investment loan					
Investment loans*	$100,000	$100,000			
Margin debt*					
Personal mortgage					
Automobile loans			$10,000		
Other mortgages		$45,000			
Personal/student loans					
Total (B)		$155,200	$11,200	$1,600	$168,000
Net worth = (A) – (B)		$977,800	$260,300	$168,900	$1,407,000

Furniture: Include furniture and appliances other than antiques and collectibles. The value you should indicate is what you would get for these things if you had a moving sale, not the replacement cost or the original cost. If you have no idea what value to assign to this category, call a couple of secondhand stores and have them give you a quote for the lot. Use the average as the value.

Pension plan: If the pension plan is a defined contribution plan, the value will be the amount on your last pension investment statement; or if you can get more up-to-date information, the value as at the date of separation.

You can usually determine the type of plan you or your spouse have by the type of statement received. A defined contribution plan usually sends a statement showing the investments selected by the employee and employer, and shows the value of the investment itself. There is no indication of the amount of retirement income the employee will receive since the amount of the pension received depends on the performance of the investments.

The defined benefit plan statement shows how much income has been earned as a retirement benefit to date as well as showing the employee's years of service and average salary. It also shows an estimate of the amount the employee will receive at age 65, or if the employee retires early.

A defined benefit plan is much harder to value. The retirement income in this plan is based on a formula that uses the employee's average salary and the number of years he or she worked for the company. Usually, the value provided by the pension plan administrators is a simple commuted value (i.e., the present value of a future stream of income) of the plan benefits, and does not take into account any of the complicating factors, such as indexing of pensions or bridge benefits. (The bridge benefit is the payment by the plan of an additional amount to an employee who retires early so that he or she is not penalized by having to start social security benefits early.) This also could add to the value of a pension. It would be best to get a qualified specialist to value such a plan. A plan which is indexed is more valuable than one that is not, since in the indexed plan, the pension payments will increase with the rate of inflation.

Company (or group) savings plan: Some companies provide their employees with stock-purchase plans, deferred profit-sharing plans, and thrift-savings plans. In most cases, the employer matches a portion of the employee's contribution. If you are unsure that you or your spouse is contributing to such a plan, you can usually find the information on pay stubs.

Registered investments: Indicate the value of any registered retirement savings plan, including locked-in plans such as 401ks, IRAs, RRSPs, and spousal RRSPs.

Non-registered investments: Include investment funds outside registered plans. These are also called open accounts, investment accounts, or cash accounts. Your broker should be able to provide more up-to-date information than the last statement you received from these accounts.

Non-registered stocks: Include stock accounts outside registered plans.

Offshore investments: Include any investments held in another country. List the value here in the currency of your country of residence.

Real estate: Include any type of investment real estate except your residence or recreational property. However, you may include any property on which either you or your spouse are shown as a registered owner.

Business: Indicate the value of any business owned by either you or your spouse, but understand that the valuation of a business can be very tricky. If you have a shareholder's agreement in place that spells out the formula for valuing the business, then valuing the business will be easy. However, this is not usually the case. In some industries there are accepted formulas that may be based on income or sales. The best way to obtain an accurate valuation of a business is to hire a business evaluator to do it for you.

Trust fund: Record the value of trust funds owned by either you or your spouse. Place this figure in the column of the trust's beneficiary; that is, the person who benefits from the trust.

Other investments: Record the value of any investment that does not fit into another category. For example, if you lent anyone money for a mortgage, or if you own a limited partnership investment, currency, gold, or anything else that qualifies as an investment, record the value here. One asset often forgotten and which may be valuable depending on couple's situation is airmiles or loyalty points.

I highly recommend that you get professionals to give you the correct values for your assets. I believe strongly that people cannot make good decisions with bad information. The old adage holds true: garbage in, garbage out. Get the best data you can. It will help you make the best decisions possible.

When you have finished entering the figures for each category, total each column to get a summary of assets (A) that are held in each spouse's name as well as those that are held jointly. Add the totals of each of these columns together to get the total of the family assets.

A brief word of warning: hiding assets can be a very costly maneuver. If your spouse discovers that you have assets that you did not disclose, the courts may award the total of that asset to him or her, instead of splitting it between the two of you, as is the case for declared assets. You should be aware that there are many ways to discover hidden assets. Lawyers and financial professionals involved in your divorce will be looking carefully at all the financial records. Business owners are usually subject to special scrutiny, as they have the opportunity to be more creative with their finances.

Your liabilities, or what you owe

The second part of the net worth worksheet examines liabilities — also known as debts. The following list contains brief descriptions of what to include for each of the categories under liabilities:

Credit cards: Indicate the total credit card debts on both your own and your spouse's credit cards. This figure will include department store cards and items purchased on a "buy now, pay later" plan.

Taxes owed: Record all taxes owed, including income tax, property tax, and sales tax (business remittance).

Lines of credit: Record the total amount owing on all lines of credit, including those of any unincorporated business you or your spouse may own.

Registered investment loan: Indicate any amount outstanding on any money you or your spouse borrowed to invest in registered plans.

Investment loans: Indicate any amount outstanding on money you or your spouse borrowed for investment purposes, except to purchase real estate.

Margin debt: Indicate the amount owing on any account held at a brokerage house to allow the purchase of investment with borrowed money.

Personal mortgage: Indicate the amount outstanding on the mortgage on your residence.

Automobile loan: State the amount outstanding on loans used to purchase a vehicle.

Other mortgages: Include mortgages against rental property, recreational property, or any other property.

Personal/student loans: Include any outstanding loans not recorded in other categories under liabilities.

Just as you did in the asset section, total the liabilities in each column to get (B), a total of the liabilities held separately and jointly. Again, by totaling the his, hers, and joint debts, you will obtain the figure for the total family debt.

At this point, you subtract (B) from (A). The result is your family's net worth. This figure represents the resources you can count on or the debt load you have to carry — vital information to have when you are facing a divorce.

Now that you have completed your net worth statement, it's time to work on the second document you will need to complete to get a clearer picture of your financial situation: the cash flow statement.

Cash Flow Statement

Too often, people set up budgets for themselves, then do not understand why these budgets do not work. Budgets often do not work because the people setting them do not truly understand their own spending patterns. Many people who go through the cash flow exercise described below are quite shocked when they discover exactly where they have been spending their money, and how much they have actually been spending.

In order to answer the question "How will I fare after my divorce?" you first have to answer the question "How have we been faring up to now?" If you know how much you've been spending on certain items up to now, you'll be better able to estimate how much you may be spending on these items after your divorce.

To do that, you must look at what you have spent in the past on various items. Perhaps the way you spent money and what you spent it on were dictated more by your spouse's lifestyle and values than your own. That's fine. Later on, you will be setting up a spending plan based on your values. However, for now, you need to know what you have actually been spending and where you've been spending it, as a family. To discover that, try the following four steps:

Step one: Use Worksheet 2 and Worksheet 3 to record your historical cash flow information. Worksheet 2 records current family income, and Worksheet 3 records current family expenses. (See Appendix 1 for Worksheet 2 and Worksheet 3.)

Step two: Decide on how many months of data you will be analyzing. Ideally, you should be analyzing a year's worth of data, but this may not be practical for you. If you do not have the time or the records to do so, you can analyze as little as three months' data and still get reasonably accurate results. Once you have decided how many months' data to use, enter that number in the "Months in period" column of the worksheets.

Step three: Obtain documentation for all the categories on both Worksheet 2 and Worksheet 3. This documentation could be pay stubs and other income statements, tax returns, bills, and receipts. Add up the individual amounts in each category listed on the worksheets and enter that figure into the "Total for period" column. For example, if you have six pay stubs for three months, total up the gross amount from each stub and enter the total of the six stubs together.

Step four: Calculate the "Monthly average" by dividing "Total for period" by "Months in period."

Income categories

The following list contains brief descriptions of what to include in each of the categories listed on Worksheet 2:

Gross employment income: Indicate the total income for you and your spouse from employment, before deductions. You will need to have this figure in any case, as it may be important in calculating child support payments.

Mandatory deductions: Indicate deductions from pay that are a condition of employment. The employee has no choice as to whether or not these deductions are going to be made from income, nor any say in the amounts. Therefore, these costs are deducted from income at source. These may include employment insurance, pension plans, social security premiums, health benefit plans, and disability insurance.

Voluntary deductions: Indicate those deductions you or your spouse may choose to have made from your pay at source. These deductions may include employee savings plans, extra income taxes, charitable donations, repayment of loans, home or car insurance premiums, benefit plans, and a host of other possibilities. This figure is recorded here for information purposes only.

Take-home pay: This figure will not necessarily be the one shown on the bottom line of the pay stub. Take-home pay, or the employee's true net pay, is calculated as gross employment income minus mandatory deductions. The items covered via voluntary deductions should be handled in the expense portion of this worksheet, since this is a choice the employee makes, which makes it discretionary spending.

Tax refund: Tax refunds are calculated as income, since the amount being deducted at source may not reflect the true amount of taxes a person pays. If someone invests in registered investments, or any financial transaction that will result in a decrease in the amount of taxes due at tax-time, or has expenses that will result in a tax refund, the refund is considered part of the family's income.

Government supplements: Include any regular payments received from the government. These may be child tax benefits, social security payments of some kind, or disability pensions. As long as it is a steady source of income, it should be recorded.

Other income: Indicate any other income here, including trust income, royalties, commissions, tips, and disability income from private insurance.

Total income: Add up the take-home pay, tax refund, government supplements, and other income, and indicate the total here.

Recording this information and performing the calculation indicated in the total income category should give you an accurate picture of how much money has been coming into your household on a monthly basis.

To understand how Worksheet 2 works, consider the following example:

John and Jenny each work. John gets paid biweekly and Jenny gets paid bimonthly. John's income is fixed, and any two consecutive pay stubs show all his deductions in a month. Jenny, however, is paid for the number of hours she works each month, and her deductions vary. They each have income information for the past three months and are confident that the past three months reflect the annual average.

John's income is easy to record. All he needs to do is to add up two consecutive pay stubs and multiply that total by 13 (there are 26 pay periods for those on a biweekly schedule) to get a year's worth of data. We know John grosses $2,400 every two weeks. His gross income will be entered as $62,400. The number of months in the period will be 12 because this number represents one year's worth of income. The figure for his average gross monthly income can be obtained by dividing $62,400 by 12, for an average monthly amount of $5,200.

His mandatory deductions for two consecutive biweekly periods equal $1,680. This amount includes income tax deductions, social service premiums, and health insurance premiums. If you multiply $1,680 by 13, that will give you the annual amount for mandatory deductions. John's voluntary contributions are $500 for the same time period, which goes toward buying company *shares. According to his pay stubs, the bottom line on his net take-home pay for two consecutive biweekly periods totals $2,620 or $34,060 for the year, taking into account the $6,500 per year he gets voluntarily deducted. Using only mandatory deductions to calculate take home pay, we see that John actually takes home $40,560 per year, which translates to $3,380 per month. The $6,500 going to the share purchase plan should be accounted for in the "savings" portion of the expense worksheet.*

Jenny's income is more straightforward. In month one, she worked 98 hours; in month two, 87 hours; and in month three, 85 hours. She feels she averages about 90 hours of work per month. She makes $20 dollars per hour.

John, because of his tax planning, usually gets a refund of about $1,800 per year. Jenny's refund usually totals about $40. They have no other sources of income. Their total disposable income is $4,973 per month.

Sample 2 shows how this information should be recorded.

Sample 2
HISTORICAL CASH FLOW: INCOME

		Total for period	Months in period	Monthly average
Income				
John	Gross employment income (A1)	$ 62,400	12	$5,200
	Mandatory deductions (B1)	21,840	12	1,820
	Voluntary deductions	6,500	12	542
	Take-home pay (C1) = (A1 − B1)	40,560	12	3,380
Jenny	Gross employment income (A2)	5,400	3	1,800
	Mandatory deductions (B2)	1,080	3	360
	Voluntary deductions	N/A	N/A	N/A
	Take-home pay (C2) = (A2 − B2)	4,320	3	1,440
	Tax refund (D)	1,840	12	153
	Government supplements (E)	N/A	N/A	N/A
	Other (F)	N/A	N/A	N/A
	Total Income (X) = C1+C2+D+E+F			**$4,973**

Expenses

Worksheet 3 — Historical Cash Flow: Expenses, looks at your historical expenses, and works much the same way as Worksheet 2. It will help you to determine the monthly averages you will need to clarify what your financial picture has been up to now.

Total the individual expenses for each category listed, for the period of time that you have chosen to analyze. It is important that you properly define the categories. To help you do so, review the following list for descriptions of what you should include in each category:

Child support payments: Indicate any payments made by you and/or your spouse to support a child from a previous marriage or relationship. Include any special expenses that the child/children may have.

Rent/mortgage payments: If renting, indicate here the amount of rent being paid. If you own your house, indicate the total amount of principal and interest you are paying on the mortgage.

Maintenance: Include maintenance fees, the cost of gardening, fixing gutters, painting, replacing towels and fixtures, kitchen equipment, linens, etc.

Property taxes: State the total amount of property taxes paid.

Miscellaneous housing: Indicate budgeted amounts for fixing major problems such as the roof, heating system, replacement of major appliances, etc.

Insurance: Indicate the cost of insurance to protect home and contents in case of theft, fire, or other disasters.

Utilities: Include the cost of heating, power, water, garbage, and alarm systems.

Cable/telephone/Internet: Include the cost of cable or satellite, home phone, cell phone, long-distance charges, and Internet connection fees.

Pet care: Include the cost of food, grooming, vet care, toys, and any other pet-related costs.

Food (groceries): Food and household supplies purchased at the grocery store.

Clothing (including cleaning): Include the cost of clothes for all family members, but do not include clothes given as gifts. Include items such as coats, gloves, hats, shoes, underwear, socks, belts, and accessories, as well as regular clothing. Also include the cost of dry cleaning.

Car loan/lease payments: Indicate the amount being paid towards a loan or a lease.

Gas: Indicate the cost of gasoline for vehicles, except recreational ones.

Insurance: Indicate the cost of automobile insurance for all vehicles, except recreational ones.

Maintenance/transit/parking: Indicate the cost of maintaining vehicles, including oil changes, tire replacement, or any other work that must be done to keep the vehicle safe and running. Indicate here also the cost of parking. If anyone in the family uses public transit, include that cost as well.

Insurance (life/DI/CI/LTC): Include any insurance premiums you pay, even if this amount comes off your paycheck. Therefore, disability insurance and group life at work will be combined with personal life insurance, critical illness insurance, long-term care insurance, or any other personal insurance premiums to give you the total that goes here.

Allowances: Indicate the amount of money that is given to children, self, and/or spouse for personal spending.

Gifts: Indicate the amount of money that is spent on gift giving to family and friends, including gifts for birthdays, weddings, anniversaries, Valentine's, Christmas, Mother's Day, Father's Day, or just for the sake of giving.

Vacations: Indicate the average cost of vacations. This amount would also include weekend trips and retreats, as well as visits to family and friends.

Tuition fees: Include any fees paid by the family for a family member who is upgrading his or her current skills and knowledge or gaining new skills, if these fees are not reimbursed by his or her place of employment.

Recreation/entertainment: Include movie admission, renting movies, eating out, or going to McDonald's, and such things as bowling, golfing, skiing, quilting, and collecting. Also include all costs associated with any recreational vehicles such as a boat or motor home, including gas, insurance, upkeep, and payments. Basically, this category includes any nonwork or nonschool activity.

Cash: Indicate the amount of cash that can't be accounted for, or cash being spent on such things as coffee, lunches, snacks, newspapers, magazines, books, CDs, and DVDs.

Personal care: Include haircuts, massages, vitamins, cosmetics, drug store items, alternative health therapies, gym fees, yoga, and any other self-care activities.

Savings/investments: Indicate all regular (annually, monthly, quarterly) savings not intended for use in the next three years, and which could be for any reason, such as travel, retirement home, cottage, or motor home.

Retirement savings: Indicate all regular (annually, monthly, quarterly) amounts specifically being saved for retirement. This money may be going into registered or nonregistered investments, as long as it is earmarked for retirement income.

Educational savings: Include any money being set aside for future education, whether for children or an adult.

Charitable giving: Include amounts donated to the church, selected charities, and causes. Also include insurance premiums if the beneficiary is a charity.

Miscellaneous expenses: Any ongoing expenses that do not fit into any other category.

Personal loan payments: Indicate fixed amount of payments on personal or student loans.

Credit card payments: Include payments to line of credits and credit cards.

Professional fees: Include all fees paid to accountants, lawyers, financial planners, or any other professional for services used.

Total expenses: Add the monthly amounts from all expense categories and place the total here.

Breakeven/surplus/shortfall: Subtract the Total Expenses indicated on Worksheet 3 from the Total Income indicated on Worksheet 2. You will be left with one of only three possible results: breakeven, which means that the money going out of your household exactly equals the money coming in; surplus, which is a positive result, meaning that you are spending less than you earn; or shortfall, which is a negative result, meaning that you are spending more than you earn.

Sample 3 is an illustration of what the Historical Cash Flow: Expenses sheet might look like once it is filled in.

Into the Future

Now that you've discovered where your money has been going, where do you go from here? Your next step is to use the information you have collected to develop a cash flow for the future. This exercise involves estimating your post-divorce expenses and income, as well as asking yourself some hard questions, such as whether or not you can realistically afford to keep the house, and what kind of insurance you'll need as a single person.

Future expenses

You looked at income first when you filled in your historical cash flow worksheets. This time you'll be dealing with expenses first when using the post-divorce estimator worksheets. The worksheet you need is the Post-Divorce Expense Estimator (see Appendix 1 for Worksheet 4). The expense categories used in this worksheet are identical to those used in the Historical Cash Flow: Expenses worksheet.

If there are children involved, there are two ways this worksheet may be completed.

The first method is to create only one set of expense numbers under your column that will include the children's expenses as well as your own. Currently, this method is most often employed because people are used to it.

The second method separates your information into two columns. The figures in the first column are based on what you would spend on your own if you had no children living with

Sample 3
HISTORICAL CASH FLOW: EXPENSES

	Total for period	Months in period	Monthly average
Expenses			
Child support payments			
Housing			
Rent/mortgage payments			
Maintenance	$1,400	12	$117
Property taxes	3,800	12	317
Miscellaneous housing	2,400	12	200
Insurance	600	12	50
Utilities	900	6	150
Cable/telephone/Internet	580	6	97
Pet care	300	4	75
Food (groceries)	1,800	3	600
Clothing (including cleaning)	300	3	100
Transportation			
Car loan/lease payments	4,800	12	400
Gas	360	3	120
Insurance	2,700	12	225
Maintenance/transit/parking	300	6	50
Insurance (life/DI/CI/LTC)	3,000	12	250
Allowances			
Gifts	500	4	125
Vacations	6,000	12	500
Tuition fees			
Recreation/entertainment	2,400	12	200
Cash	600	3	200
Personal care	400	3	133
Savings/investments	6,500	12	542
Retirement savings			
Education savings			
Charitable giving	600	12	50
Miscellaneous expenses	300	3	100
Personal loan payments			
Credit card payments	300	3	100
Professional fees	300	3	100
Total Expenses (Y)			**$4,801**
Surplus(+) / Shortfall( ) = Total Income (X) minus Total Expenses (Y) Monthly			$172

you. The figures in the second column are based on the extra costs you incur as a result of the children living with you. When you are planning for life beyond children, this method is more effective. Especially if the children are teenagers, it allows you to recognize and plan for your needs when the children leave home. It is also effective if your children have special needs, such as daycare, private school, university costs, or health-care costs, since these costs may inflate what is seen as your cost of living.

Use whichever method is most appropriate to your situation and with which you are comfortable.

Here is an example of how to enter data. If you own a house, are you or your partner planning on staying in the house? If so, then all house-related expenses will be entered into that partner's column. If one or both partners are going to rent, put the estimated rent in the appropriate column. If you are separating out the children's expenses, and you need a two- or three-bedroom apartment to accommodate the children, the difference between the cost of a one-bedroom apartment and the family apartment will go in the children's column in the blank beside "Rent." The key to using this worksheet effectively is to be realistic. If you have typically spent $500 per month on food for the family and your spouse has moved out, you will not suddenly be spending $250 per month on food. Chances are, your food bill may drop by only 20 percent to 25 percent. Of course, if you are changing your eating habits drastically, the impact on your food bill may be larger.

We will continue with the example of John and Jenny, and their daughter Jill who is 15. Jill plans on leaving home as soon as she legally can, which is at the age of 18. She plans to go live in Australia with her boyfriend. Until she reaches 18, John will have to pay $500 per month as basic child support payments.

Sample 4 shows that Jenny wants to keep the house, since there is no mortgage on it. Jill will be living with her, so her expenses are included with Jenny's. The expenses are shown as monthly. We are making the assumption that John will be renting, and his expenses are being estimated as well to give a more realistic picture of the resources that will be available for sharing after the divorce. You will notice that John is no longer saving through his payroll plan.

Sample 4
POST-DIVORCE EXPENSE ESTIMATOR

POST-DIVORCE EXPENSE ESTIMATOR			
	Hers	Children	His
Child support payments			$500
Housing			
Rent/mortgage payments			1,000
Maintenance	$117		
Property taxes	317		
Miscellaneous housing	200		200
Insurance	50		25
Utilities	125		
Cable/telephone/Internet	75		75
Pet care	25		
Food (groceries)	400		250
Clothing (including cleaning)	100		50
Transportation			
Car loan/lease payments			400
Gas	80		80
Insurance	125		100
Maintenance/transit/parking	50		25
Insurance (life/DI/CI/LTC)	125		125
Allowances			
Gifts	75		50
Vacations	300		200
Tuition fees			
Recreation/entertainment	150		150
Cash	100		100
Personal care	100		50
Savings/investment			0
Retirement savings			
Education savings			
Charitable giving	25		25
Miscellaneous expenses	100		100
Personal loan payments			
Credit card payments	100		
Professional fees	50		50
Total expenses	**$2,789**		**$3,555**

Almost always, the first worksheet is done trying to maintain the current lifestyle. Comparing this expense sheet to the Historical Cash Flow: Income worksheet, something becomes immediately clear. Given the current lifestyles, with John's take-home pay of $3,380 per month and Jenny's at $1,440 per month, there is not enough money to go around after the divorce. Your true post-divorce income picture will become clearer when you do the Post-Divorce Income Estimator worksheet (see Appendix 1 for Worksheet 6). This just gives you an initial feel for your finances.

The difference between your Post-Divorce Expense Estimator worksheet and the Post-Divorce Expense Estimator with Child Expenses Separated (see Appendix 1 for Worksheet 5) that you will be completing is that you will be estimating your expenses solely according to your own values. You should base the numbers you enter into the Post-Divorce Expense Estimator worksheet on a blend of your historical spending, your own priorities in life, and what you consider realistic. Perhaps you and your spouse, when you were together, used to spend a lot of money on entertainment and recreation. However, you have always been more concerned with financial security than entertainment. Now you have the opportunity to allocate what *you* feel is a reasonable amount to entertainment and recreation and a larger amount to debt reduction or retirement savings to meet your personal goal of financial security.

Sample 5 shows what the Post-Divorce Expense Estimator with Child Expenses Separated worksheet would look like in a situation in which the child's expenses were separated from the parent's expenses. In this scenario, both parents would be renting. The cost in the child's column is the additional cost that would be incurred for an apartment with another bedroom, driving the child around, and other child-related costs.

Your first pass at Worksheet 4 or Worksheet 5 may reflect your ideal lifestyle, and that's fine for now. However, you can determine if that lifestyle is workable only after you look at your income sources, which is the next part of this exercise.

In my practice as a financial planner specializing in divorce, I have frequently been asked why I don't simply create the initial expense estimate to fit the expected income. My reasons are manyfold. First, it is important that you know the kind of lifestyle that will make you happy. Second, if you can't afford that lifestyle now, at least knowing what you want sets up the

Sample 5
POST-DIVORCE EXPENSE ESTIMATOR
With Child Expenses Separated

POST-DIVORCE EXPENSE ESTIMATOR WITH CHILD EXPENSES SEPARATED			
	Hers	Children	His
Child support payments			$500
Housing			
Rent/mortgage payments	$1,000	$350	$1,000
Maintenance			
Property taxes			
Miscellaneous housing	100	50	100
Insurance	25		25
Utilities	75	50	75
Cable/telephone/Internet	100	30	100
Pet care			
Food (groceries)	300	150	300
Clothing (including cleaning)	100	100	100
Transportation			
Car loan/lease payments	250		300
Gas	80	40	100
Insurance	125		120
Maintenance/transit/parking	50		30
Insurance (life/DI/CI/LTC)	85		100
Allowances		100	
Gifts	75	40	75
Vacations	100	75	100
Tuition fees			
Recreation/entertainment	150	75	250
Cash			
Personal care	100	50	50
Savings/investment			
Retirement savings	200		200
Education savings		150	
Charitable giving	50		100
Miscellaneous expenses	100	50	100
Personal loan payments			
Credit card payments			
Professional fees	80		30
Total expenses	**$3,095**	**$1,310**	**$3,255**

basis for a long-term plan to obtain it. Third, if you know what you want and why you want it, it puts you in a better negotiating position. Lastly, estimating your post-divorce expenses before estimating your post-divorce income can help to prevent a poverty mentality from setting in. Unfortunately, too many women, in my experience, base their lifestyles on *what they expect to get, not on what they need*. The result is that many of them remain poor during their working years and in retirement end up living below the poverty line.

Future income

Worksheet 6, the Post-Divorce Income Estimator, is also quite similar to the Historical Cash Flow: Income (Worksheet 2). One difference, though, is that it has room for only one income, rather than two. Another difference is that it has two more categories as income: spousal support and child support. The child-support column will include any known special expenses, such as childcare, that your ex-spouse will be paying.

Sample 6 shows you what this worksheet may look like once you fill it in. It shows Jenny's post-divorce income, if she continues her current work pattern.

Sample 6
POST-DIVORCE INCOME ESTIMATOR

	Annual	Monthly average
Income		
Gross employment income (A)		$1,800
Mandatory deductions (B)		360
Voluntary deductions		
Take-home pay (C) = (A – B)		1,440
Child Support payments (D)		500
Spousal Support payments (E)		
Tax Refund (F)		
Government Supplements (G)		
Other (H)		
Total income (X)=(C+D+E+F+G+H)		$1,940

Go with the flow

After you have entered the details of potential expenses and income, you total the numbers to get total expenses and total income. Subtract the total expense from the total income to give you your cash flow. Is your cash flow going to be positive, neutral, or negative?

If it is going to be positive, that's great. You now have one less source of stress.

If your cash flow is neutral, then as a precaution, you might want to look at the suggestions below for people with negative cash flow. It would be wise of you to make a few changes to nudge your cash flow into solidly positive territory when it is so close to being there already.

If your cash flow is negative, don't despair. There are several things you can do:

- First, look at your income sources. Is it possible to increase your income? What can you do? Do you need retraining? Do you need to upgrade your skills or take a refresher course? How long will it take to do these things? How much will it cost? Can you reallocate your resources to make a difference in your income?

- Second, look at your expenses. Is there any category in which you can trim back? What are your needs as opposed to your wants? Needs are those things that are necessary to life or those situations that, if not addressed, will worsen (e.g., if the roof is not fixed, it will cave in). Wants are those desires that can, in fact, wait for a while. If a want is not fulfilled, it will not have a negative impact on your health or well-being in the near future (e.g., if you are used to having a massage weekly and must cut back to monthly, you would still be okay).

  When looking at cutting back on expenses for each category, ask yourself what you would gain or lose by the cutbacks. How much are you willing to cut back? How committed are you to this cutback? If you are willing to cut back only on paper but not in real life, you will find yourself in real financial difficulties.

- Once you have decided where your cutbacks will be, you should create a new expense worksheet with the changes you have made to see how the situation looks. Continue doing this until you have a scenario with which you can live.

- The last area for you to examine is your other resources, besides income. If you are asset rich and cash poor, you may have to look at the impact of converting some of your assets into cash. Keep in mind, however, that converting assets into cash is a very serious decision. It means you are using up your capital. Your ability to recover will depend on your age and your ability to earn future income. If you cannot replace the capital you are consuming, and you are fairly young, your retirement lifestyle may be at stake. In order to preserve capital, you must look at the value of the converted assets on an after-tax basis. See a financial professional who is familiar with investments and the tax laws in your area for advice.

To Keep or Not to Keep the House: That Is the Question

One of the largest assets many divorcing couples have is their home. "Can I keep the house?" is probably the question uppermost in the mind of at least one member of the couple.

Many women, at the onset of the separation, decide they want to keep the house. Sometimes, it is because of the children. Often, it is because they do not feel they will ever be able to afford to buy one on their own, and a house, for many women, is equated with security. They will give up pension benefits, investments, and make many other concessions just to keep the house.

Quite often, this decision is poorly thought out. Women who insist on keeping the house frequently leave themselves asset rich and cash poor. They have the house, but a huge percentage of their resources go into keeping it. The end result is that many are forced to sell the house, usually within five years, because they do not have the cash needed to support both themselves and the house.

Look at the following example:

When Joyce and Ryder separated, Joyce wanted to keep the house. They were both working and making good salaries. They had no children. In order to keep the house, Joyce traded Ryder her registered investments. Neither had a pension plan at work. Her settlement at the end of the divorce was $15,000 in investments (shown below in the first row of the "Liquid Assets" column in Table 1), a house valued at $270,000, and a mortgage against the house of $190,000. The net equity in the house ($270,000 minus $190,000) is the $80,000 shown in the "Net Real Estate" column. Joyce has take-home pay of approximately $31,000 per year (shown in the "Net Salary" column).

To maintain the house, Joyce cut back on all her expenses to a bare-bones standard of living of $22,063 (shown under the "Living Expenses" column), which excluded her mortgage payment. The mortgage payment of $13,937 is shown under the "Mortgage" column. Despite her cutbacks, between her living expenses and her mortgage payments, Joyce still has a negative cash flow of $5,000 in her first year (shown in the "Cash Flow" column). She had intended the $15,000 to be her emergency funds, but as you can see on the table below, her liquid assets are being depleted because of the shortfall. If nothing else changes, Joyce's emergency funds will be used up within four years. At that point, if she wishes to keep the house, she must start accumulating debts to cover the shortfall. The only reason Joyce could afford to keep the house is that the growth of the equity in the house (which also results in growth of net worth) would allow her to borrow against it, which in return, increases her cost of living since she now has to pay interest on the accumulated debt. Joyce is definitely asset rich and cash poor. Owning the house dictates a very restricted lifestyle for Joyce.

In the above example, Joyce could at least afford to keep the house. It is more common that after a few years, the person who kept the house is forced to sell because the debt load is too high to carry.

There are two very important things to consider in this situation.

Table 1

Joyce's Financial Sheet	Version							
	Age	Net Salary	Living Expenses	Mortgage	Cash Flow	Liquid Assets	Debt	Real Estate Equity	Net Worth
Notes	44	3.00%	3.00%	25 years		5.50%	7.50%	3.00%	
	44	$31,000	$22,063	$13,937	($6,000)	$15,000		$80,000	$95,000
	45	$31,930	$22,725	$13,937	($4,732)	$10,825		$90,387	$101,212
	46	$32,888	$23,407	$13,937	($4,455)	$6,888		$101,186	$107,875
	47	$33,875	$24,109	$13,937	($4,171)	$2,801		$112,417	$115,018
	48	$34,891	$24,832	$13,937	($3,878)		($2,276)	$124,100	$121,824
	49	$35,937	$25,577	$13,937	($3,577)		($7,897)	$136,255	$128,358
	50	$37,016	$26,345	$13,937	($3,265)		($13,081)	$148,905	$135,824
	51	$38,126	$27,135	$13,937	($2,946)		($17,814)	$162,073	$144,259
	52	$39,270	$27,949	$13,937	($2,616)		($22,083)	$175,783	$153,700
	53	$40,448	$28,787	$13,937	($2,276)		($25,874)	$190,061	$164,188
	54	$41,661	$29,651	$13,937	($1,926)		($29,173)	$204,936	$175,763
	55	$42,911	$30,541	$13,937	($1,566)		($31,966)	$220,434	$188,469
	56	$44,199	$31,457	$13,937	($1,195)		($34,235)	$236,587	$202,352
	57	$45,525	$32,400	$13,937	($813)		($35,967)	$253,427	$217,460
	58	$46,890	$33,372	$13,937	($419)		($37,145)	$270,986	$233,842

(From Divorce Pro software. Used with permission of the College of Divorce Specialists.)

First, Joyce is not able to save any money for her retirement, and she gave up what she did have (i.e., her registered investments) to keep the house as part of her divorce settlement.

Second, if you look closely at the above table, you will see that even though Joyce's income is increasing, it is increasing at the rate of inflation only, and her expenses are also increasing at the same rate. Joyce is still living in scrimp-mode years after the divorce, just to maintain the house. This is what it means to be asset rich and cash poor.

Don't Forget Your Other Assets

The house question may be foremost in your mind, but it is likely you and your spouse have other assets too. You will be faced with the question of how to split these assets. The more knowledge you have about them, the better equipped you will be to answer that question.

Pensions

A pension that is earned during the marriage is a family asset, and as such, is subject to the property division rules of the jurisdiction in which you live. The amount of the pension to be divided depends on two key factors. The first is the type of pension, and the second is the portion of the pension that was earned during the marriage.

Types of pensions

Most pensions will be one of two types: a defined contribution plan or a defined benefit plan.

In a divorce, one part of the pension division formula is the value of the investments on the date of separation or the date of the divorce. For the defined contribution plan, this value may be obtained from the statements provided by the pension administrator. For the defined benefit plan, an initial estimate may be obtained from the pension administrator. A more accurate valuation may be obtained by hiring an actuary, a pension evaluator, or a financial planner trained in pension valuations.

Usually the pension administrators of defined benefit plans send out a letter showing the commuted value. Unless the defined benefit is a "non-integrated, flat rate" plan, such as those set up for some trade unions, the value may not be accurate due to the reasons mentioned earlier in this chapter.

Proportion of pension earned during marriage

The other part of the pension-division formula is the proportion of the pension that was earned during the marriage. Consider the following example:

If Jane and Mark were married for 15 or more years, and Mark was in his company's pension plan for 15 years, then 100 percent of his pension was earned during the marriage. The pension in this case would normally be split 50/50 between Jane and Mark. However, if Mark had been in the plan for 15 years, and he and Jane were married for only 10 years, only two-thirds of the pension was earned during the marriage. Only 66 percent of the plan will be a family asset and therefore subject to division, and Jane would be entitled to 33 percent of Mark's pension.

There is one more decision the couple has to make concerning the disposition of the pension: When is the money to be received?

They could choose to have a lump sum of the pension paid out immediately, as part of the settlement. If the pension plan allows this option, then the appropriate amount is transferred to a registered plan (usually governed by the same rules as the issuing pension plan) in the receiving spouse's name, and invested to earn future income. If a transfer out of the plan is not allowed, or if the parties prefer, the pension owner could trade an equivalent amount in other assets for the shared value of the pension. It is important when this type of trade is being done, and the trade is between assets that are taxed at different rates, that only after tax values are taken into consideration. This ensures assets being traded are valued in a fair manner. One example of this would be that capital gains are not taxed in the same way as earned income. Consult a local accountant or financial planner so that you understand the rules for your jurisdiction. This option is used when the parties want a clean break with as few financial ties between them as possible.

The second option is to receive the proportional amount of the divorced spouse's retirement benefit only when the pension owner starts to receive his or her pension. This option is used when one spouse has spent time and energy building the other's career, which is now about to take off. This option allows the non-pension owner to participate in the future growth in income. However, it is also a riskier option for the one who does not own the pension. He or she is at the mercy of circumstances outside his or her control, such as when he or she can start receiving the pension.

When it comes to dealing with pensions during your divorce, consider all your options carefully, and don't be afraid to enlist the help of a financial planner or an actuary. In the long run, you may not only be saving yourself money, you may also be making it for yourself too.

Registered retirement investments

Most households now have some form of registered retirement investments, such as 401Ks, IRAs, and RRSPs. In a divorce, all investments accumulated during the marriage, regardless of who is the owner of record, are considered family property.

One key point to remember when it comes to splitting investments is that registered (meaning tax sheltered) investments are not worth the same amount of non-registered investments. This is because taxes must be paid on the investment when it is taken as income. To be fair in the division of assets, you must take tax consequences into consideration. The following example illustrates some of the consequences:

Review the Joyce and Ryder example above. Assuming that both would be in a 20-percent tax bracket at retirement, $100,000 of their registered retirement assets would be worth $80,000 after-tax dollars. If Joyce lives in Canada, where personal homes are tax-exempt, she would have to trade Ryder $100,000 in registered investments for $80,000 worth of his equity in the property for the after-tax values to be equal.

Dividing liabilities

When liabilities are attached to assets, usually the value used for division is the net asset value. Net asset value is the value of the asset minus the liability. For example, if a house is valued at $300,000 and the mortgage is $100,000, the net asset value of the asset to be divided as family property is $200,000.

When liabilities are by themselves, such as a line of credit, or charge cards, then the amounts would be divided according to the same formula for dividing assets.

Emergency Funds

For most people, divorce is a financially draining experience. There is the cost of setting up a second household. There are legal and other fees. Your finances are bound to be in a state of flux as you try to separate which assets and liabilities you will keep from those your spouse will keep.

It is essential that you have an emergency fund or safety net in place. Conventional advice is that you should have enough money to see you through three to six months of expenses in your emergency fund. This fund may be cash, a clear line of credit, or a visa card with no outstanding balance.

However, should none of these options be available to you,

try to arrange to have a family member or friend be your banker, should you find yourself in a situation in which you really need additional funds. Knowing that you have access to emergency funds can free you to work on the real issues.

One good idea is to write out a definition of what "emergency" means to you and stick to it! Don't spend that money on anything outside your definition. This ploy may very well keep you from nickel-and-diming your emergency funds out of existence. Try to look for creative solutions to the many small, often seemingly urgent, expenses.

Protecting Yourself and Your Loved Ones

Even once you have dealt with the splitting of assets and liabilities, you still have many other issues to consider. These will include such things as your power of attorney, Will, beneficiary designations, and insurance. A little attention to these issues now can provide you and your loved ones with a measure of security.

Powers of attorney

A power of attorney is a legal document in which you bestow upon a person the power to make legal financial decisions for you, when you are unable to do so for yourself. (**Note:** For the purposes of this document, this person is called an attorney although he or she is not usually a lawyer.) There are two types of power of attorney: restricted and unrestricted.

The restricted power of attorney is one that comes into effect only in the case of you being stricken with a mental or physical disability, or on some other condition specified in the power of attorney. A restricted power of attorney may also deal with very specific assets.

An unrestricted power of attorney is one in which there is no limit to what the person you have appointed as your attorney can do. Also, since there are no specific conditions under which it becomes effective, it is effective from the date you sign it.

A power of attorney is not automatically invalid on separation or divorce.

If you had an unrestricted power of attorney during your marriage, in which you had appointed your spouse as your attorney, you may want to revoke it immediately upon separation, or even before you discuss separation. With this document, your spouse may legally do anything you can do, including accessing your non-joint bank accounts and investments.

It is a good idea to either revoke your power of attorney, or change the person whom you designate as your attorney to someone you trust to act on your behalf. You may wish to contact a lawyer for advice.

Wills

When you separate or divorce, review your Will along with your other important legal documents. Doing so may allow you to ensure that your estate will pass to those you want it to go to, and not to your ex-spouse.

During the separation process, your soon-to-be-ex spouse is still legally your spouse. You can change your Will any time you please. However, be aware that even if you change your Will at this time, if you were to die within the first year of separation, especially if division of property between you and your spouse had not been completed, your ex-spouse would have a very strong claim against your estate. That claim, during the separation period, diminishes with time. After the divorce is final, there is no official claim. If you have separated and want to ensure that your spouse does not inherit any portion of your estate, see a lawyer for advice.

However, even your divorce will not automatically render the Will you had during your marriage invalid. If you had a Will during your marriage in which you left your estate to your spouse, you must make a new Will if you wish to leave your estate to someone other than your ex-spouse. If you fail to do so, the Will you had in place during your marriage takes effect upon your death — provided you have not remarried.

You should also revisit your Will to change the executor and/or trustee if you had named your ex-spouse as such. You may also want to deal with any property that is not considered matrimonial property at this time.

Beneficiary designations

At some point during the separation process, usually as soon as the monetary issues have been addressed in your separation agreement, you should be looking at changing the beneficiary designations on your registered investments, company benefit plans, and life insurance.

By designating a beneficiary on your registered investments and life insurance policies, you ensure that these assets will not fall into your estate when you die. They go directly to whomever you have designated. Even your Will may not override a designation, and that can cause unexpected problems:

Jim and Anna had been separated for four years. They had completed their property division. Jim kept his RRSP intact, and Anna kept hers. Following his divorce Jim began living with Sara. He did not want to get married again, but he and Sara did want to take care of each other should either of them die. When they had been living together for about 18 months, they each had Wills made up in which each left the other everything. No mention was made of any specific life insurance policy or RRSP.

Jim died in a car accident five months later. Sara got the house they lived in and the spousal RRSP to which she was a beneficiary. Anna got the larger RRSP and the $100,000 insurance policy, because Jim had never gotten around to changing the beneficiary designations from Anna to Sara.

The Value of a Career

There is one major asset that is not officially recognized by the courts. This is the value of a career and the assets associated with it. When calculating a spouse's income, it is also important to value such things as life, disability, and health insurance; vacation pay, sick pay, education, and training; stock options; company car; travel allowances; expense accounts; and any other benefits that confer a monetary benefit, directly and indirectly. Consider a situation where one spouse has the ability to purchase life insurance at group rates for both spouses. After the divorce, the spouse without the benefit plan must replace that insurance with regular premiums which can be three or more times the cost of the group coverage. This is an area that is only now being recognized as a value within a marriage.

Insurance

Your separation and divorce will affect your need for insurance, and this section examines all types of insurance. Each type of insurance has its own purpose. Home (or property) insurance covers the loss of physical property in case of theft or fire. Life insurance pays out a benefit to your designated beneficiary on your death. Disability insurance and critical illness insurance take care of living expenses in case of illness or accident. Long-term care insurance is designed to protect the quality and dignity of your old age. You should include all your insurance costs as expenses in your cash flow statement. Each type of insurance is described below.

Home (or property) insurance

In the drive to cut expenses when a couple separates households, home insurance is usually a casualty. Unless you can afford to replace all of your possessions, including clothes, pots and pans, and furniture, you need insurance.

If you are keeping the house, you may want to review the policy to see if you need the same level of coverage you had during your marriage. If your spouse had a home business, you may not necessarily need to keep the business rider on the policy. Find out if your policy has any special riders and consider whether or not you still need those riders.

If you are moving from your house into an apartment or condo, then fire insurance will cost a lot less, since it will cover only the contents of your apartment, not the building.

Do not skimp on the liability insurance that is part of your homeowner's or tenant's policy. This coverage will pay damages if someone is injured while on your property and sues you as a result. Liability insurance is probably the least expensive portion of your coverage.

Life insurance

If you needed life insurance during your marriage, consider carefully whether or not you will continue to need it when you are single again. Life insurance is used to protect those who are dependent on your income, to pay off debt and taxes on your death, or to leave a legacy.

Many times during a marriage, the individuals have life insurance policies issued under the same policy number. During separation, these policies should also be separated.

This is not usually a problem if there were two individual policies in which both members of the couple were joint owners. Send a letter to the insurance company signed by both of you, or send a copy of your separation agreement, requesting that the policy ownership be changed to each of you individually.

If, however, you had a joint first-to-die policy or a joint last-to-die policy, the situation becomes more complicated. Depending on your insurance company, you may not be able to separate the policy, and each of you may have to apply for a new policy. If a number of years have elapsed since you obtained the original policy, keep in mind that you may now be uninsurable due to health, or that it may be more expensive for you to obtain coverage now, due to your age. Insurance cost is dependent on age and health; therefore, you must do a realistic evaluation of how much coverage you need.

Disability insurance

Disability insurance will pay you a monthly income if you are unable to work due to an illness or injury. The coverage will continue only for as long as you are disabled or until your benefits run out.

A newly single person may find he or she has different financial considerations than a long-married one does. When you are married, if you have a prolonged absence from work, your spouse's income is there to take care of the basics. But a single person in the same situation faces an uncomfortable question: where will the money come from? If you do not already have disability insurance at your place of work, consider obtaining private insurance.

It may seem costly to you to have this insurance, but the cost of not having it is greater. It takes only six month of illness to wipe out years of savings if you have no other source of income to see you through that time.

Unfortunately, not everyone qualifies for disability insurance. You must be working and making a minimum amount per year in order to qualify. In addition, some professions are excluded or very expensive to insure because of the history of claims made by those in that profession. An insurer will also take your personal health history into account before granting you coverage.

Critical illness insurance

Critical illness insurance is quite unlike disability insurance. This particular kind of insurance pays you to survive a major illness such as a heart attack. On the first occurrence of one of the illnesses specified in the policy, the insurer will pay out a lump-sum amount to you, after a qualifying period.

You may use this money for any reason. You might wish to pay off the mortgage, go on a trip, buy some investments, or get treatment. There may be other ways you would choose to spend this money.

Unlike disability insurance, for which you must be working to qualify for coverage; critical illness insurance may be purchased even if you are not earning an income.

Critical illness insurance can provide very important coverage for singles with mortgages and debts. If you are at all concerned about protecting your financial security in the event of a serious illness, check out critical illness coverage. Today, the number of people surviving heart attack, heart disease, and cancer is increasing. However, the financial setbacks of such illnesses are also increasing.

Personal health history and family history will be very important in determining if you qualify for critical illness insurance.

All policies are not created equal, though. The range of what is covered is quite astonishing. Ask for quotes from more than one company and have the broker explain the differences in the definitions of the covered illnesses. When it comes to choosing this type of insurance, price should not be the deciding factor; getting the coverage best suited to you should be.

Long-term care insurance

The article on divorce and aging quoted in Chapter 1 indicated that "it is divorced female boomers who are in danger of being the major victims [of divorce] in old age, at least financially."

The implications of that statement are enormous. In an aging society where governments are trying to cut costs, it is up to individuals to make at least some provision for their own care and comfort in their old age.

Long-term care insurance provides a daily benefit for the policyholder if he or she is unable to perform some of the basic activities of daily living for himself or herself. The benefit is the amount of insurance a person buys. For example, a benefit of $100 per day will provide an income of $36,500 per year. Insurance may be purchased for a specific number of years or for an unlimited number of years.

It may be purchased for care in a facility only, or for care both at home and/or at a facility. There are many add-ons and variations to the basic concept. The earliest you can qualify for coverage is age 40.

For many divorced persons, disposable income is a challenge, even during their maximum earning years, and the cost of the premiums for long-term care insurance may seem an unnecessary burden. If you fall into this category, however, you must ask yourself the following question: If you can't afford long-term-care premiums while you are working, how can you afford the cost of care when you are not?

If your marriage was long standing, and you find yourself without much of a support network following your divorce, you may want to consider getting long-term care insurance. You may even negotiate to have this coverage paid for as part of your separation agreement.

As in using any professional, when buying insurance, find a broker who has your best interests at heart. He or she should shop for the best policy to fit your needs. Don't be shy in asking for several quotes, options, alternatives, and understandable explanations.

Now that you've worked through some of the money issues involved in separating from your spouse, you should be able to see your post-divorce financial picture taking shape. However, there are other issues that may affect your finances that should be addressed in your separation agreement, which, after all, is often the document on which your settlement will be based. The next chapter deals with the composition of the separation agreement.

Chapter 6

Separation Agreement Considerations and Separation Preparedness

In separation, deadly as poison,
in union, brimming with nectar.
What, did fate make my love
out of both equally?

— Hla Stavhana (c. 50 AD), South Indian king, Prkrit poet

A separation agreement is a document that lays out the terms and conditions for separation and eventually divorce between you and your partner. For the agreement to be valid, both you and your spouse must agree to it and sign it. Regardless of which path to divorce you choose, one of the best things you can do to help ensure your security is to get a good separation agreement in place as soon as you can.

I did a survey of 100 divorced persons, both men and women. Their situations ranged from no children, no property to extensive property and dependent children. Ninety-eight said that if they had to do it over again, they would get the separation agreement started as soon as possible.

There is one key to writing a good separation agreement: clarity, clarity, clarity. Be specific in your language. Any term or clause in the agreement that may be open to question will be interpreted in ways you cannot even begin to imagine. And having no agreement at all can be very costly.

Here is one person's story:

Tom and Joanne were married for six years and had no children or significant property.

Joanne was employed as an executive assistant, making about $60,000 per year. Tom was a struggling reporter making about half that amount. Tom came home from work one day to find Joanne gone.

He was devastated. He threw himself into his work, and had no further contact with her.

A year later, Tom was served with papers for Joanne's support. During their year apart, she had quit her job, and now she needed financial help. She alleged that Tom had made promises that, in fact, he never had made.

Tom immediately went to see a lawyer. He was told he could fight, but it would be a costly process. Eventually, Tom settled out of court by getting Joanne to accept $5,000. Obtaining that settlement cost him an additional $2,000 in legal bills, all of which came from his hard-earned savings of the past year.

In hindsight, it is easy to see that if Tom and Joanne had a written agreement at the time of separation saying neither one was entitled to financial support from the other, this situation would not have occurred. Tom did not think they needed one, because they had no property or children and the issue of support seemed silly at the time.

Many people delay getting a separation agreement drawn up because they believe that they must have all issues settled first. In other words, they think it must be all or nothing. This is not true. You and you spouse can create an interim or temporary separation agreement at the time at which you separate. Doing so does not mean that you have no areas of disagreement. It simply documents those issues on which you have agreed. For example, your agreement may document physical custody of the children, visitation schedules, sharing of expenses during the separation period, temporary spousal support, or a host of other issues. This agreement is built upon one issue at a time, until all the issues are resolved and the final agreement is completed and signed.

From a financial planning point of view, there are several issues discussed below that may be covered by the separation agreement with which you want to take special care.

Protection for Children

Protection for children must be addressed at two levels. The first is financial protection. However, once you have worked out your support arrangements for your children, you should also look at using life insurance as a means of protecting the children's income stream in case of the death of the payor. Your agreement could state that for the duration of the child-support period, the paying parent will maintain a life insurance policy for an adequate amount.

It is not enough that the receiving parent be the irrevocable beneficiary (i.e., the beneficiary cannot be changed without the beneficiary's permission) of the policy. The policy owner should be the receiving spouse as well. If the receiving spouse owns the policy, he or she will be notified if the policy is cancelled by request or due to non-payment of premiums. After the paying parent has died, it is too late to find out that the policy no longer exists.

See to it that the insurance policy is in place before the separation agreement is complete. This way, if the paying parent turns out to be uninsurable, other clauses may be added to the agreement to ensure that the estate of the paying parent will assume responsibility for child support.

Some parents do not like to designate the receiving spouse as the beneficiary of a large lump sum of money. If such is the case for you, there are two ways you might handle the issue. First, you can arrange that the death benefit from the insurance policy be paid out as an annuity. (An annuity is a fixed monthly payment for the period of time selected.) If you want to allow for more flexibility and discretion, you may set up the beneficiary as a trust for the children and name a trustee to administer the support payments.

You should also give some consideration to what might happen in case the paying parent becomes seriously ill or is disabled. Consider the example below:

Joe was 34 years old and was the separated father of three children. He was paying the prescribed amount of child support. His separated wife was working only part-time because of the ages of their children.

Joe was in a very bad car accident, which left him severely disabled. He got a large settlement from his insurance company, but in the five years following his accident, the cost of his care ate up most of it.

Things got to the point that he could not continue to pay child support. His separated wife, the untrained mother of three young children, had to go on social security. None of the jobs for which she was qualified would allow her enough income to cover the cost of childcare.

Could this situation have been handled in the separation agreement? I don't know. It may depend on the laws of your jurisdiction and it is something to discuss with your lawyer.

Special Expenses

One issue that can become very contentious between separated or divorced couples is that of special expenses. Special expenses are those expenses that cost more than $100 per year and which are incurred on behalf of the child. These may include childcare, school trips, sports equipment, extracurricular activities, dental or other health-care costs to name only a few. Usually, the cost is shared proportionally between the parents, according to income. If both parents are making approximately the same income, the expenses will be shared fifty-fifty. Again, it is quite possible for one party or the other to use this issue as a tool for control or revenge — which is all the more reason for you to make certain things are spelled out clearly in your separation agreement. The following example illustrates the dangers of not being precise in your agreement:

Jenna and Randy had a 16-year-old daughter, Cathy, who attended private school. In addition to child support, they had been sharing all her expenses on a 70/30 basis. Randy was self-employed and paid 70 percent of the special expenses due to his income, which was higher than Jenna's income.

Cathy's grade 10 class was going to Europe for the summer. Jenna committed to the trip without consulting Randy. He had just bought a new home and his business was in a downturn. His portion of the cost for the school trip ($7,000) was a hardship on him.

It caused a great deal of conflict between them for a while, which in turn had a negative effect on Cathy.

In your agreement, describe in as much detail as you can under which circumstance both you and your spouse will agree to any special expenses. As best you can, list the things you would both consider extraordinary expenses. I have seen circumstances in which dad considered shoes to be covered under child support payments, but mom considered the $150 pair of Nikes to be an extraordinary expense.

Many agreements do not include any clauses stating when special expenses must be paid or whether or not there is a penalty for not paying special expenses promptly. Such a situation means that the receiving parent may have to resort to getting a lawyer to "encourage" the other party to pay — a costly procedure — or may not collect at all. Since one parent is incurring the cost and having to carry the other parent's share until the other parent pays, it is wise to lay out in your agreement a reasonable time frame for the reimbursement of special expenses. You and your spouse should also agree on an appropriate penalty for late payment; for example, interest on the cost of the expense. Make sure, though, that your agreement states clearly if, when, and how much interest may be appropriate.

Children's Education

One of the things that sometimes falls through the cracks of a separation agreement is the funding for the children's post-secondary education. Your agreement should specify who is responsible for which educational expense, and should also deal with the disposition of any funds meant but not used for educational purposes.

Ensure also that your agreement is exact regarding financial responsibility for adult children still attending school full time. At what point should such responsibility terminate? Of course, if either parent wishes to continue supporting his or her children after the specified date, he or she may certainly do so. However, it is in your interest to have a stipulated date.

Parenting Plans

Once you have had children together, and if you love your children and intend to be involved in their lives, co-parenting is something you will share with your ex-spouse for the rest of both of your lives. This partnership will never end. Therefore, it is in the best interest of the children and both parents to develop a parenting plan. This can provide your children with the emotional security they need, which is reassurance they are still loved by both parents. Parenting does not end when the children go off to college or get married. Parents become grandparents; they are involved in all the triumphs and tragedies of their children's lives to the day they die.

A parenting plan allows you to discuss how you will handle discipline problems, family problems, sharing of economic help that may be needed by the children, and many other issues.

While not directly a financial planning issue, access is often an area of major conflict that can result in significant financial hardship owing to legal costs. You can avoid this trouble by ensuring that your parenting plan and your agreement defines your arrangements regarding your children on weekends, school holidays, vacations, birthdays, religious holidays, or any other days that have significance to either of you. It should also clearly state who will pick up the children and drop them off. In addition, it should detail what both you and your ex-spouse consider a reasonable time frame for giving notice that you want to negotiate varying these arrangements.

Spousal Protection

The separation agreement also contains the details of property division and spousal support.

It should contain any formulas or actual numbers for the division of assets and liabilities. It should detail dates by which assets must be transferred to the other spouse, and liabilities paid off or assumed.

If there is going to be spousal support, then the separation agreement would describe the terms of conditions under which the support will be paid, as well as the amount and duration of the payments.

Besides financial protection, any terms relating to personal safety will also be written into this document.

The separation agreement is the key to the divorce process. A well-crafted agreement may make the difference between a civilized or a nightmare experience after the divorce. It and the parenting plan live on long after the marriage is over. If both you and your spouse sign an agreement clearly stating your expectations and the consequences of various actions, there will be little room left for interpretation. Should a conflict arise, your chances for a simpler, less costly resolution will be all the greater.

If one of the parties does not live up to his or her obligations in the agreement or divorce decree, then the other party has some options. For example, many states and provinces have agencies that will help receiving parents enforce child support payments. Some agencies will also help enforce spousal support, but it is quite likely the couple may end up in court over this issue. If personal circumstances change for either party, they may apply to the courts to change the terms and conditions of the agreement or the decree.

Again I stress that you do not have to agree on all the issues before you create a separation agreement. You can draw up an interim agreement that includes the issues on which you have agreed, and you can keep updating the agreement as you resolve other issues.

See Appendix 2 for tips on preparing for separation and information on settlement negotiations.

Chapter 7

Starting Over: Your New Financial World

You have many choices.
You can choose forgiveness over revenge, joy over despair.
You can choose action over apathy.
You hold the key to how well you make the emotional
adjustment to your divorce and consequently how well
your children will adapt.

— Stephanie Marston (20th century),
US parent educator, author

Once your divorce is over, your life takes on new dimensions. You will find yourself starting over again in a world that is no longer familiar to you. You have to learn to be a single parent who is not truly a single parent, since you have to consider your ex-spouse in decisions concerning the children. You will have to cope with dating again, while the scars from your divorce are still fresh. You will find yourself wanting financial security, right after your financial world has been rocked to its foundations.

Unlike the separation period, when your future financial situation was unknown, now, with the property division and support arrangements in place, you know the resources with which you have to work.

Post-divorce is a time for planning ahead and rebuilding — either on your own or with a new partner.

Financial Planning Considerations

Financial planning starts with you knowing what you want. The following is a list of questions you should ask yourself to discover your wants and needs:

- What will it take to make me feel financially secure?

- What kind of lifestyle do I need to make me happy, both now and in retirement? Why? Are there other, non-material ways to satisfy my emotional needs?

- What will I do after I retire?

- How much money will I need to retire the way I would like to?

- Given my current assets and circumstances, what will it take to build my retirement savings to the level I want it to be?

- Am I willing to restrict my current lifestyle to ensure my future lifestyle?

- What am I willing to give up?

- Realistically, when do I think I will be able to retire?

- What is my health like? Are there any degenerative problems in my family health history that I should be concerned about?

- If I need help as I age, what kind of system do I need to have in place for physical, emotional, and financial support?

- In case of an emergency, on whom can I depend for financial support?

- Who is depending on me for financial support?

- How can I provide for my dependents if I die? If I became seriously ill?

- How important is it to me that I help my children financially with their education? Wedding? Home purchase? Etc.?

- How secure is my job? Do I like my job?

- What do I need to do to get a job I like and which will support me?

- What do I have to do to ensure financial security if I should re-marry?

- What do I want to do — or need to do in the next year — and what would it cost? What do I want or need to do in the next two, three, five years?

Answering these questions will help you clarify your goals. Like most people, you may find it difficult to accommodate all your financial desires at the same time. Therefore, you may need to decide the order of importance of your goals. It is easier to start working on your top two or three goals first. Once you are on your way to achieving those goals, or once you have a sustainable plan in place for achieving them, you can review your list and go on to the next goal.

You can do a great deal of financial planning yourself. However, it pays to find a trustworthy financial planner to work with you. Even if you have the interest and time to do your own financial plan, a good planner brings insights of many years to the table, as well as the experience and knowledge necessary to implement the plan. Since you may not be an expert in investments, insurance, or debt reduction, cash-flow management, estate planning, tax planning, and retirement planning, a good advisor would be invaluable. He or she should help you deal with your most urgent needs (for example, debt management or cash-flow management), or help you find the most tax-efficient way to start generating an income on which to live. A comprehensive plan may evolve over a number of years, as your situation changes. However, regardless of the plan being comprehensive (all inclusive) or modular (working on one part at a time), you should have a personalized, written financial plan.

Regular monitoring and updating of your plan is as important as the initial plan itself. Life is not static, so your plan should not be written in stone. When very little is happening in your life, the plan may be reviewed *at least* annually. Definitely, it should be reviewed whenever there is a change in circumstances that will affect you financially. Some of these circumstances may be getting married or moving in with someone, having a baby, losing or changing jobs, illness, major purchase, getting an inheritance, or any one of a number of events.

What follows below is a discussion of the areas your plan should include.

Debt reduction

If your divorce resulted in you carrying a debt load, make certain your plan has a debt-reduction strategy. The plan should look at your resources and your debts and determine the timeframe within which you can reasonably expect to become debt free. It should include strategies and show the benefits of options such as debt consolidation and reducing interest rates. It will usually suggest a budgeted monthly amount to pay off debts; and set up an action plan showing which debts are to be paid off first, second, and third, etc. A good plan will also include little rewards for reaching certain goals, so that you can celebrate your progress.

Savings

Savings, in this context, are not the same as investments. Savings here mean accumulating money from normal cash flow to be used for some specific purpose. Savings goals may include an emergency fund to absorb loss of wages, to buy a car, to get a down payment for a house, to have a baby, to accumulate a retirement fund, or any one of a thousand other things.

Saving is very difficult for many people, especially in our instant-gratification society. Today, it is so much easier to purchase the new sofa you want on credit and pay for it over the next three years rather than saving for it and then purchasing it. What is amazing in our disposable society is that sometimes the credit card payments outlive the useful life of the item purchased. The financial cost to you, the consumer, is enormous. By squandering your resources in seemingly small amounts, you prevent yourself from reaching your big goals. For example, you purchase a television for one thousand dollars and pay for it with a credit card on which the interest is 18 percent. By making payments at 3 percent of the original balance ($1000), or $30 per month, the card will be paid off in three years. What is the final cost of the television? $3,127 dollars. On a credit card on which the interest rate is only 9 percent, the final cost would be $2,543 dollars.

When asked to save $50 per month, many on a tight budget will say no. But when asked if they could save two dollars daily or the price of two cups of coffee, the majority said yes. No matter how tight your budget, the best way to save is to *pay yourself first*. This concept is not a new idea. However, for many it is not easy to do. One suggestion is to have automatic withdrawals come out of your bank account each month on the day after your paycheck is deposited. Another is to save your pocket change at the end of the day, and then at month-end, take it to the bank. The trick to this one requires putting the change jar out of sight, and making a commitment that when it goes into the jar, it is as good as gone.

Investments

Investments are where you keep the money you have saved or are saving. Investment goals are differentiated more in terms of their characteristics rather than purpose. For example, the primary investment goal for your savings for a house down payment would be safety of your capital, while your goal for your retirement savings might be growth of capital. If you are not working, the goal for your divorce settlement assets might be to provide a steady stream of income with some growth. Each of these goals will result in a different investment recommendation. When selecting investments, carefully consider your altered circumstances, your goals, and the length of time the money is to be invested to make sure that your needs are met by, or are compatible with, the type of investment you choose. Verify that the investment fits your personal comfort level. It does not matter how big a return you can get on your money: if you can't sleep at night because you're worrying about it, it is the wrong investment for you.

If you know you'd like to purchase a home after your divorce, your financial plan should address various methods for purchasing a house — by cash or by mortgage — and show the impact each of these options will have on your overall financial picture.

Risk management

Risk management is nothing more — or less — than looking at what could go wrong in your life and putting in place contingency plans to handle these situations. The following questions speak to emergency situations that are not uncommon and which could happen to anyone. What plans do you have in each case?

- What happens if you lose your job?

- Where can you get money in an emergency?

- Are you likely to need long-term care in the future?

- Do you have disability insurance in case you can't work?

- If you can't work due to a life-threatening illness such as cancer, where will the funds for living come from?

- Are you starting a home-based business? Do you have the appropriate riders on your homeowner's policy?

- Do you need life insurance to cover your financial obligations in case of death? Having life insurance coverage to pay off the mortgage on your death will ensure that your dependents have some assets or a place to live. Having additional coverage to pay for living expenses means that someone else will not have to assume the financial burden for your dependents.

- Do you face a special risk that should be addressed?

Having a contingency plan in place for these common risk situations will provide you with peace of mind.

Beneficiary designations

As mentioned in Chapter 5, you should change your beneficiary designations at the time of your separation. However, now that your divorce is complete, double-check that all beneficiary designations on your life insurance policies, registered plans, employment benefits, etc., reflect your new status.

Power of attorney

At the time of your separation, you likely revoked your power of attorney if your designated attorney was your spouse. Now is the time to have your power of attorney redone. Consider inserting a clause that states which events can trigger your power of attorney. (A triggering event is one that activates the power of attorney, such as mental infirmity, your absence from the country, or physical incapability.) Discuss the pros and cons of triggers for your power of attorney with a lawyer or attorney.

Will

If you have not already done so, this is a good time to get your Will redone. Remember, divorce does not invalidate your existing Will. You may wish to give special consideration to leaving assets to your minor children. Consider, also, the terms and conditions of any trusts in your will. The three major issues in your will, apart from the disposition of bequests, are your appointment of the executor, the guardian, and the trustee. The executor is the person who ensures that the terms and conditions of the will are met. The guardian is the person who has physical custody of the dependents. (Appointment of a guardian is only an issue if you have sole custody of the children, since in joint custody situations, your spouse will be the automatic guardian.) The trustee is the person who looks after the investment and disbursements of the money left for the children. It is always wise to separate the guardianship from the trusteeship, to protect both the guardian and the children.

Marriage or cohabitation agreement

If you are beginning another relationship, do give serious consideration to putting an agreement in place. It is very important to your future financial security. See Chapter 8 for a detailed discussion of such agreements.

Children and your cash flow

For the sake of your cash flow, don't get into a bidding war with your ex-spouse for your child's affections. That's a sucker's game. Children are masters in the art of manipulation. Children are quite capable of playing one parent off against the other in order to get material goodies, and that ploy could easily blow your budget out of the water.

You may want to involve children from the age of ten in the family finances. When shopping for back-to-school clothes, you can ask them what they need and how much they think it will cost. If the amount is reasonable, give them the money to pay for the clothes themselves, so they'll see how far that sum actually goes. When dealing with older children, give them your budgeted amount and tell them what it is expected to buy. They can choose to buy whatever they like, but they will not get another clothing allowance for, say, four months.

You may find it very hard as a parent to stick to this plan when you see your children not dressing the way you would like them to, due to a lack of clothes. Keep in mind, however, that you are teaching your children a life lesson. This is not about you; it is about them.

Your financial plan is a roadmap for your security. In your post-divorce world, your plan can give you not only a sense of stability, but also a sense of direction. You'll know where you are going and how you plan to get there. You can also look forward to a tremendous sense of satisfaction as you achieve your financial goals, one by one, all on your own.

C h a p t e r   8

Remarriage Preparedness

A bride at her second marriage does not wear a veil.
She wants to see what she is getting.

— Helen Rowland (1875 – 1950), US journalist

Many of the problems in a marriage may be prevented by the creation of a marriage or cohabitation agreement. Should you find yourself contemplating getting married again, consider having such an agreement in place before proceeding. In the United States, 75 percent of women and 80 percent of men remarry within five years of getting a divorce. Unfortunately, second marriages are at a higher risk for divorce than first marriages.

Applying the principles discussed in this chapter may have one of two possible outcomes: a good relationship could become better, since both parties are on the same page regarding their expectations; or the transition out of a bad relationship may be made more smooth, since many of the contentious details will already have been addressed in the agreement.

Separation preparedness is like earthquake preparedness. You try to put everything in place so that if it happens, you can deal with it effectively, but you hope it does not happen in your lifetime.

Marriage Contracts/Pre-nuptial Agreements/Cohabitation Agreements

A marriage contract or agreement is also referred to as a domestic contract, a pre-nuptial agreement, or a cohabitation agreement. The language used to refer to the document will vary according to the circumstances. The agreement is called a cohabitation agreement when it is drawn up for a common-law couple. For a married couple in Canada, it is called a marriage contract. In the United States, it is called a pre-nuptial agreement and is usually negotiated before the marriage. However, a marriage contract may be drawn up before or at any time during a marriage, and a cohabitation agreement may be drawn up at any time before or during cohabitation.

A major difference between a marriage contract and a cohabitation agreement is what happens in the absence of one. In a marriage, if no contract exists, then the division of property will be governed by the property division legislation for that jurisdiction. The same is not true for common-law relationships. At this time, only a very few states or provinces have the same rules for both types of relationship. In most cases, common-law couples are not subject to property division legislation when there is a breakdown in the relationship. It is important that you find out the rules in your part of the country.

For the purposes of this book, I will use the term "agreement" when referring to all types of agreements.

The primary intent of an agreement is to document — outside the court system, and before there is a problem with the relationship — the agreement between the couple on division of their property. These contracts used to be the norms in arranged marriages of old. Since the advent of "love" matches, however, it seems that common sense and love do not mix. Today, there is the perception that to discuss such mundane matters as money handling or personal expectations before a marriage puts an undue strain on a relationship driven by passion. Yet it is these very issues that contribute to so many divorces.

A big factor for many people is the legal cost for preparing an agreement. However, the cost of getting an agreement in place is only a fraction of the cost of divorce proceedings.

Most fights in a relationship are about unmet expectations, including those related to finance. It follows then, that a key component of a long and happy partnership is getting the expectations of both parties on the table right at the beginning.

Agreements are all about expectations. The agreement lays out each party's expectations and states what obligations each will have in the case of a triggering event, such as death or divorce. The agreement may be about a specific asset or may encompass a total lifestyle.

Of course, you don't expect your relationship to fail. No one does. But then again, no one truly expects to die young, have a house fire, or become seriously ill, but they still purchase insurance. So too, should couples consider having one of these agreement drawn up, in case the unthinkable becomes reality.

Statistically speaking, the chance of a person getting divorced is much higher than that of dying before age 65, experiencing a house fire, or suffering a major illness before age 50. Consider that the divorce rate for first marriages is about 33 percent; and for second and subsequent marriages, it is about 50 percent.

Frequently Asked Questions

In considering having an agreement drawn up, a couple will have many questions. Here are some of the most frequently asked questions, along with answers:

1. **Are agreements only for those who have assets to protect?**

   No. Agreements are used to protect against unfair loss resulting from being in a relationship. This loss may be the loss of assets, income, or a loss caused by the assumption of a burden of debt. Consider the following example:

Joe and Sally were together for five years. They met at university and fell in love. Joe was studying to be a doctor, and Sally was in nursing. It was not long before they moved in together. They did not explicitly discuss their future, but they expected to get married someday.

Their tuition and living expenses were high so Sally decided to go to university only part-time, so that she could get a job to help out financially. She thought that when Joe graduated, he would be making enough money for her to return full-time and finish her degree. She supported them for four years. During that time, they purchased Joe a motorcycle to make it easier for him to get around. It was in his name.

When Joe went into his internship, he met someone else. His relationship with Sally ended.

Sally was left struggling to complete her degree on her own. She ended up with a $15,000 debt at graduation.

If Joe and Sally had been married, Sally may have been entitled to compensation for her contributions to the family unit, such as some financial support to complete her own education. However, married or common law, the best strategy would have been for them to create an agreement at the outset of their relationship. An agreement outlining the financial obligations of both parties in the event of a relationship breakdown would have left Sally in a much better financial situation.

Look at another example:

Cheryl and Mark got married after knowing each other for two years.

Mark was a professional from a well-to-do family, and Cheryl did not expect to have any financial problems after the wedding.

They had a wonderful wedding to the tune of $35,000, paid for by Cheryl, before the wedding, on her charge cards.

Mark was unfaithful to Cheryl soon after their honeymoon. Within three months they were separated and filing for divorce.

Cheryl was humiliated and wanted out of the marriage with the least amount of hassle. It took her four years to pay off the debt for the wedding.

In this case, property division laws would have been of no benefit to Cheryl. She had two strikes against her: the length of the marriage (very short), and the debts having been accumulated in her name prior to the marriage. There would have been little chance of getting Mark to share the cost of the wedding, even had she gone to court.

The better solution in this case would have been for Mark and Cheryl to have drawn up a marriage contract stating that they were both responsible for the wedding costs.

Still another example:

A well-to-do widow with three children, Cassandra was entering into a marriage with a divorced gentleman. She loved the man and envisioned a long and happy life with him.

Her advisors suggested a pre-nuptial agreement to protect her and her children. She went along with their advice, despite her own reluctance.

The marriage ended within the year.

With the pre-nuptial agreement in place, the financial separation between them was not an issue.

---

2. **Do cohabitation agreements only apply to heterosexual couples?**

   Cohabitation agreements are legally enforceable contracts between consenting adults. Sexual orientation has nothing to do with the validity of the contract.

3. **What can be covered by an agreement?**

   An agreement may cover only specific issues such as financial arrangements, or it can be as comprehensive as the couple wants. Taken to the extreme, an agreement can cover the handling of —

   • property;

   • support arrangements;

- life insurance;

- budgeting and credit;

- child care;

- family and social obligations;

- sex and birth control;

- household duties;

- daily routine and courtesies (i.e., dinner time and calling if you will be late);

- relationship building (daily talk time, getaways, etc.);

- emotional trust (never lying or cheating);

- personal attire and grooming;

- hobbies, recreation, celebrations, and vacations;

- roles and responsibilities; and

- inheritances and gifts.

Be aware, however, that terms other than those addressing financial arrangements, and ownership and division of property, assets, and liabilities, may not be enforceable in court. In other words, any terms detailing responsibilities for household chores and routines may not be legally enforceable, since there are no laws governing those things. However, it can be useful to include such terms in your contract simply to document the personal arrangements between you and your spouse on these matters. You must also understand that one thing you absolutely cannot do in an agreement is sign away the rights of a child, such as the right to child support.

4. **What could make an agreement signed before the wedding invalid?**

The major reason why a pre-nuptial agreement could be invalid is it having been signed too close to the wedding date. The term used to describe this situation is "ink on the wedding dress," meaning that it could be argued that pressure may have been applied by one spouse on the other to get him or her to sign the agreement. It could be argued that the other partner, in order to avoid the embarrassment of being left at the altar, signed a document he or she would not otherwise have signed.

5. **What could make any of these agreements invalid?**

    Any agreement may be invalidated due to the following circumstances:

    - The agreement contains terms or conditions that could promote a divorce or separation, such as an agreement to pay extremely generous spousal support should the relationship break down.

    - Pressure or threats were used to get one of the parties to sign.

    - The agreement has terms or conditions that could leave one of the parties destitute.

    - One party lied materially about the value of his or her assets when the agreement was created.

    - One party used undue influence to get the other party to sign. (To avoid this, each party should consult, and pay for, his or her own lawyer. Independent legal advice is necessary to ensure the validity of the agreement.)

    - Some of the terms and conditions of the agreement were frivolous. An example might be that one party is to be recompensed financially if the other party forgets an anniversary.

6. **Under what circumstances would you recommend an agreement be put in place?**

    An agreement should be drawn up whenever a person starting a relationship wants to ensure fairness. Specifically, I would recommend that an agreement be in place in the situations listed below:

    - All common-law (heterosexual or same-sex) relationships, since they fall outside of property division rules in most jurisdictions.

- Relationships in which one party owns substantially more assets or earns significantly higher income than the other.

- Second marriages, when there is a need to protect children of the first marriage.

- To protect a specific asset, such as a matrimonial home.

- When one party in the relationship owns a business, in order to protect the other business partners' interests. It could be a condition of partnership that each of the partners has a living-together agreement in place with his or her spouse that protects the business. The agreements should specify what happens in relation to the business ownership in case of death or divorce.

These agreements are not written in stone. If you do have one, review it periodically to make certain it still applies to your circumstances. Without this review and update, the longer you are in a relationship, the less value the original agreement will have.

Another point to remember is that parties to the agreement are not obligated to enforce it, as written. If a party wishes to either be more generous to the other, or not to enforce the contract to his or her benefit, that party may do so with no negative consequences.

What If There Is No Agreement?

In the absence of an agreement, here are some other steps you can take to protect assets long before you ever even contemplate a divorce. This information gives you choices. The problem I have encountered in my practice is that many people do not know the potential consequence of their decisions. If you have a general idea of what may happen as a consequence of making a certain decision, you are at least making an informed choice.

Incoming assets

One of the very first things you can do to protect yourself is get a value of your personal net worth at the time of your marriage. Division of property usually addresses assets accumulated during the marriage. However, it can be very hard to establish the original net worth of individuals who have been married for a long time. Assets are co-mingled and used for family purposes and generally tend to get lost in the shuffle. For division of assets to be fair, both you and your partner should have net worth statements done at the time of marriage and filed away with your important papers. This statement does not have to be fancy. A simple, dated list of assets and liabilities will do, if you can back it up by copies of statements.

There is a plus side to putting together a net worth statement. A discussion with your partner before the wedding about financial resources may trigger a discussion on money management styles and preferences. If you know what your spouse-to-be is like and you both go in with eyes wide open, you may have fewer financial conflicts. Just do not expect to change your prospective partner to fit your style. That is a recipe for disaster.

Matrimonial home

The matrimonial home is the only exception to the value of assets brought into the marriage. If your only asset at the start of your marriage is a house (fully paid for or not), that dwelling becomes the matrimonial home if you and your spouse live in it. Your spouse is automatically entitled to share in its value, should the marriage break down. To maintain the value of your pre-marriage assets in case of a breakdown of your marriage, you may want to sell the existing home and invest the money realized from the sale in an account in your name only. This money is now your asset and should not be used for family purposes.

You may purchase a new home — using money other than that realized from the sale of the first home — which will become the matrimonial home. This way, your net worth at the start of the marriage remains intact, and it is the new matrimonial home that will become subject to asset division in the event of a divorce.

Be aware that in many jurisdictions, for the purpose of property division, you may have more than one matrimonial property. For example, a family may have three matrimonial properties: the family home, the family cottage, and the winter home in Arizona.

Gifts, inheritances, and insurance settlements

When it comes to splitting assets, couples often make the source of the funds used to purchase family assets an issue. This is especially true if the source of the funds was a gift, an inheritance, or a personal-injury award of some sort. It is seldom an issue to the courts, however. To the courts, a family asset is an asset used for the benefit or enjoyment of the family, and as such, it will be subject to the division of assets. The source of the funds used to acquire that asset is irrelevant to the courts in determining the division.

Therefore, to protect assets gained from an inheritance, gift, or insurance settlement, you must do some planning as soon as you receive the money.

Gifts

Today, it is very common for parents or grandparents to help members of the younger generation own a home by gifting them with money. Some parents want their children to have their inheritance early, while they (the parents) are still alive. Although they may love the in-law, seldom is their intent permanently to gift the in-law with at least half the money. Yet that is usually the end result

What happens to that money as a result of a marriage breakdown depends on how the gift was structured and/or how the money was used:

John and Kim got married seven years ago.

When they started a family and wanted to buy a house, both sets of parents agreed to help them financially. John's parents gave them $30,000 for the down payment.

Kim's parents gave them the rest, as a registered mortgage against the property.

The mortgage was at zero percent, with no payments due. It was a balloon-payment mortgage. (A balloon payment is one in which the entire amount is due and payable at a certain date.)

John and Kim recently separated.

The net equity in the home is family property and therefore will be split equally between them. The net equity is calculated as the market value of the house, less the mortgage.

That means the down payment gifted by John's parents will be subject to property division. John's parents are horrified. The down payment was a gift to their son, not to his wife.

Kim's parents are secured creditors because of the mortgage. They will get all of their money back, which they can give to their daughter later.

The surest way for parents or grandparents to protect their gifts is to request that a marriage contract be drawn up as a condition of the gift. This agreement must then detail what would happen to the gift in case of a divorce or untimely death of the person to whom the gift was made.

If the amount of the gift is substantial, the gift donor may want to register a mortgage or lien against the property being purchased with the money he or she has gifted. However, the gift donor would have to ensure that adequate provisions are made in his or her will regarding how the mortgage or loan is to be handled by the executor. Again, to avoid conflicts with family-law legislation in your area, you should consult a lawyer.

Inheritances

Inheritances are a tricky business. In some jurisdictions, the donor may legally specify that the inheritance is not to be part of the family assets. In others, it is the use of the inheritance that determines whether it is family property or not, as illustrated by the following example:

Jane and Samantha received equal inheritances of $150,000.

Jane used her money to pay off the mortgage on the cottage she and her husband purchased five years before, where the family spent most weekends. A few years later, in the divorce, the cottage was considered matrimonial property and divided equally. Jane's $150,000 inheritance was absorbed into family assets.

Samantha, however, purchased an apartment in her name only. She rented out the apartment. She had any excess income placed in a savings account and she used that money to treat herself from time to time. When she got a divorce, her apartment was not considered family property since the source of the funds she used to purchase it was her inheritance and it was never used for the enjoyment or benefit of her family.

Parents' ability to protect their heirs' inheritances depends on state or provincial laws. Parents concerned about their children's current or future marriage who want to protect their children's inheritances should consult a lawyer.

Insurance proceeds

In most jurisdictions, personal injury awards and life insurance proceeds are also excluded property in property division. As with inheritances and gifts, to keep the exclusion, if it is allowed, you must exercise care in how you invest and use the funds. If the funds are co-mingled with family funds or used to purchase family property, the funds or property could be included in family assets. Keep accurate records, leave a paper trail, and you can save yourself problems.

Joint assets

As part of their estate planning, many elderly persons transfer property into joint names with their married children. Their purpose is to pass the home upon their deaths directly to their heirs, without estate taxes or probate fees. Many parents who do this are unaware that in the absence of any agreement between their child and his or her spouse, their (the parents') property (real estate, bank accounts, or investments) may be considered a family asset for division of property purposes, since it was acquired after the marriage. This misguided attempt to avoid estate taxes or probate fees can become very costly. During the parent's lifetime, in a divorce proceeding, their son or daughter's spouse may go after the assets their son or daughter holds jointly with them. The best way to avoid this problem is for parents not to put property into joint names with their married adult children. If for some reason the parent wishes to do this, there should be an agreement in place between the spouses specifically stating that this joint property is not part of the married child's matrimonial assets.

Banking issues and money handling

In this age of plastic and instant gratification, it is very important that you establish a credit history of your own.

Very often, when people get married, they start setting up joint accounts and take out joint loans or joint mortgages. Doing so is fine until there is a divorce or death. The spouse with the lower or no income may find that he or she does not have a credit history, and may find that he or she has difficulty purchasing a home, car, or even getting a credit card.

It is vital, then, that during the marriage, each partner builds up a credit rating. Always maintain a credit card in your name only. Ensure that you use the credit card at least a couple of times each year. If you do so, your credit file will build itself. But keep in mind that a bad credit rating is worse than no credit rating at all; so make your payments on time. If you have a partner who is careless about such matters, get rid of as many joint debts as possible, and look after the ones you can't get rid of. Don't let your partner ruin your credit rating.

Financial Planning Considerations in Marriages

Going into any marriage (first, second, or third), you should consider how you wish to handle joint obligations such as household expenses, children's education, as well as personal obligations such as protection for your family and your own hobbies and spending.

There is no right or wrong way to handle money in a marriage. Find a way that works for you *both*. I have seen situations in which each party deposits his or her paychecks into separate accounts and split the expenses 50/50. They contribute equally to any joint projects and maintain their own retirement savings. I have also seen variations in which the expenses are shared proportionally. I have seen this model work very well, and I have seen it not work at all, depending on the couple and how much each party was earning.

I have seen couples who have only joint accounts. If the marriage was a spender/saver union, the arrangement caused a lot of friction because of the parties' differing spending styles. One variation of this model is joint accounts with each party having an allowance he or she can spend or save as desired.

Your financial considerations in a marriage will be no different than your financial considerations for being single with dependents. The difference is that the two of you have to agree on what is best for you and your blended and/or extended families. Your discussions should address what each of you need to feel secure in terms of money handling and bank accounts; your retirement, as in the kind of lifestyle you want and how you will both contribute to achieving it; your need for the various types of insurance; emergency funds; your wills and power of attorney; how you will handle requests for help from your children; and many more personal issues.

A Word of Caution

It is regrettable that second and subsequent marriages have a higher divorce rate than first marriages. Nonetheless, to use an old cliché, forewarned is forearmed. By all means, remarry if you wish to do so. But you should always do your financial planning as if you will have only yourself to depend upon.

Afterword

Divorce is never easy, regardless of the circumstances leading up to it. However, it need not be the financial disaster it has the reputation of being. As difficult as it might be, if one does some cool thinking and planning, based on information and knowledge, then one's life post-divorce may be all the better for the lessons learned during the ordeal

Worksheets

Worksheet 1
NET WORTH

Assets	Ownership				Household Totals
	Original Value*	Joint	His	Hers	
Personal					
Bank accounts					
Savings					
Life insurance cash value (not death benefit)					
Residence					
Recreational property*					
Collectibles/valuables*					
Vehicles					
Furniture					
Investments					
Pension plans					
Company savings plan					
Registered investments					
Non-registered investments*					
Non-registered stocks*					
Offshore investments					
Real estate*					
Business*					
Trust fund					
Other investments					
Total (A)					
Liabilities					
Credit cards					
Taxes owed					
Lines of credit					
Retirement investment loan					
Investment loans*					
Margin debt*					
Personal mortgage					
Automobile loans					
Other mortgages					
Personal/student loans					
Total (B)					
Net worth = (A) – (B)					

Worksheet 2
HISTORICAL CASH FLOW: INCOME

		Total for period	Months in period	Monthly average
Income				
	Gross employment income (A1)			
	Mandatory deductions (B1)			
	Voluntary deductions			
	Take-home pay (C1) = (A1 − B1)			
	Gross employment income (A2)			
	Mandatory deductions (B2)			
	Voluntary deductions			
	Take-home pay (C2) = (A2 − B2)			
	Tax refund (D)			
	Government supplements (E)			
	Other (F)			
	Total Income (X) = C1+C2+D+E+F			

Worksheet 3
HISTORICAL CASH FLOW: EXPENSES

	Total for period	Months in period	Monthly average
Expenses			
Child support payments			
Housing			
Rent/mortgage payments			
Maintenance			
Property taxes			
Miscellaneous housing			
Insurance			
Utilities			
Cable/telephone/Internet			
Pet care			
Food (groceries)			
Clothing (including cleaning)			
Transportation			
Car loan/lease payments			
Gas			
Insurance			
Maintenance/transit/parking			
Insurance (life/DI/CI/LTC)			
Allowances			
Gifts			
Vacations			
Tuition fees			
Recreation/entertainment			
Cash			
Personal care			
Savings/investments			
Retirement savings			
Education savings			
Charitable giving			
Miscellaneous expenses			
Personal loan payments			
Credit card payments			
Professional fees			
Total Expenses (Y)			
Surplus(+) / Shortfall( ) = Total Income (X) minus Total Expenses (Y) Monthly			

Worksheet 4
POST-DIVORCE EXPENSE ESTIMATOR

POST-DIVORCE EXPENSE ESTIMATOR			
	Hers	Children	His
Child support payments			
Housing			
Rent/mortgage payments			
Maintenance			
Property taxes			
Miscellaneous housing			
Insurance			
Utilities			
Cable/telephone/Internet			
Pet care			
Food (groceries)			
Clothing (including cleaning)			
Transportation			
Car loan/lease payments			
Gas			
Insurance			
Maintenance/transit/parking			
Insurance (life/DI/CI/LTC)			
Allowances			
Gifts			
Vacations			
Tuition fees			
Recreation/entertainment			
Cash			
Personal care			
Savings/investment			
Retirement savings			
Education savings			
Charitable giving			
Miscellaneous expenses			
Personal loan payments			
Credit card payments			
Professional fees			
Total expenses			

Worksheet 5
POST-DIVORCE EXPENSE ESTIMATOR
With Child Expenses Separated

POST-DIVORCE EXPENSE ESTIMATOR WITH CHILD EXPENSES SEPARATED			
	Hers	Children	His
Child support payments			
Housing			
Rent/mortgage payments			
Maintenance			
Property taxes			
Miscellaneous housing			
Insurance			
Utilities			
Cable/telephone/Internet			
Pet care			
Food (groceries)			
Clothing (including cleaning)			
Transportation			
Car loan/lease payments			
Gas			
Insurance			
Maintenance/transit/parking			
Insurance (life/DI/CI/LTC)			
Allowances			
Gifts			
Vacations			
Tuition fees			
Recreation/entertainment			
Cash			
Personal care			
Savings/investment			
Retirement savings			
Education savings			
Charitable giving			
Miscellaneous expenses			
Personal loan payments			
Credit card payments			
Professional fees			
Total expenses			

Worksheet 6
POST-DIVORCE INCOME ESTIMATOR

	Annual	Monthly average
Income		
Gross employment income (A)		
Mandatory deductions (B)		
Voluntary deductions		
Take-home pay (C) = (A − B)		
Child Support payments (D)		
Spousal Support payments (E)		
Tax Refund (F)		
Government Supplements (G)		
Other (H)		
Total income (X)=(C+D+E+F+G+H)		

Tips on Preparing for Separation and Settlement Checklist

Tips on Preparing for Separation

If you are at the point at which separation between you and your spouse is imminent, there are some steps you can take to help you avoid complications and unnecessary problems. Prepare as if you are facing a worst-case scenario. The more you prepare, the less likely you are to be unpleasantly surprised. If you find after the fact that you did not need as much preparation, you'll have done no harm. It's far better to be over-prepared than to be caught without the information you need and have no way of getting it.

1. If you do not already have one, apply for a credit card to start building your credit rating. A credit rating is extremely important if you want to be able to purchase a home or a car, or even get a loan on your own.

2. Try to work out where you'll be financially after the divorce. Do a cash flow statement of potential income and expenses. Use the information and worksheets in Chapter 5 to help you do this.

3. Open your own bank account and start saving some emergency money. This way, if your joint account is emptied, you will not be left stranded. You may also feel more secure knowing that you have the cash to cover a few months' living expenses. If you yourself are taking money from the joint accounts, joint line of credit, or joint investments, consider very carefully the impact it will have on the tone of the divorce.

4. Get copies of statements of your joint bank accounts, loans, lines of credit, credit cards, and investments. It is important that you know what the balances were at the time of separation. It is not unheard-of for one party to max out the family cards, liquidate investments, or empty bank accounts as a form of revenge soon after separation is discussed.

5. As soon as the separation is effective, even if you and your spouse are still living in the same house, get an interim separation agreement in place.

6. Cancel as many joint credit instruments (credit cards, lines of credit) as possible. Doing so protects you from a spousal spending spree or credit sabotage. If you cannot cancel these instruments, send a letter to the creditors, along with a copy of the separation agreement, if available, immediately upon your separation. Outline the situation and inform them that you will not be responsible for debts accumulated after that date. Do not continue to use joint credit. If you do, it will be very difficult for you to divide your portion of the credit from your spouse's.

7. Take dated pictures of each room in the matrimonial house and of all physical assets. The photographs will not only prove the assets were real; they will also show the quality and the condition of those assets. This documentation could be valuable in trying at a later date to establish the value of your assets.

8. Check out your safety deposit box or any other location at which you keep your important papers. Get your copies of all important documents, including insurance policies. The truism is that if it is in your safety deposit box, it is important to one of you.

9. Get copies of your spouse's tax returns (the entire document) for at least the past two years, if you can. Slips filed with the tax return may give you valuable clues to the existence of hidden assets.

10. If you don't believe you really know your financial situation, keep an eye on the mail that comes in addressed to your spouse. Copy the name and sender's address of any mail that looks like it came from a financial institution.

11. Try to work out what your life after divorce will be like. Do you need to upgrade your education to earn more or become employable? Start looking at your options as soon as you can. Research the job market and keep the information you find. It could affect your divorce settlement.

12. Get some books and learn the basics of separation and divorce. If you understand the process and know what to expect, you will be less bewildered and frustrated during the process. Do not rely on descriptions from friends who have gone through divorce, as a friend's experience may have no bearing on yours.

13. Do you think child custody may be an issue? Start keeping a parent's journal. Record things from the child's point of view, including your children's activities, both your and your spouse's participation in the children's lives and activities, and your and your spouse's consideration for the children's welfare. After the separation, continue to record visits and significant events. Try not to be biased in your recording.

14. Get some professional legal advice before you move out of your home. In some jurisdictions, leaving the home may have an impact on custody and/or your rights to the family home. However, if necessary, get out without legal advice if physical or other abuse is occurring in the home.

15. You need a network for emotional support. Family and friends are best, but not always available. No matter whose choice it was to leave the marriage, it is hard on both parties. If you do not have a support system in

place, you can usually find community or church divorce support groups to help you through this time.

16. Give someone whom you trust all of the information you have gathered for safekeeping. This way, it will be there when you need it.

17. Don't even start thinking of using your divorce to punish your spouse. You will most likely end up punishing yourself.

18. Don't expect fairness from the system. Your idea of fair and the law's idea of fair are not the same. Since the law is based on trying to be fair to as many people as possible, it is seldom fair to any one in particular.

19. Hard as it may be, keep in mind that the best way to preserve your assets is to try to stay out of court. The more set you are in your position, the harder it will be to come to an acceptable compromise. It is also important for you to look at the long-term effects of any decisions you make on both you and your spouse.

Settlement Checklist

Below is a list of items that you and your spouse should cover or at least discuss during your negotiations. This list is by no means exhaustive, nor will all the items apply to everyone. It is intended to help you highlight issues that are important to you and your situation.

1. Disclosure of all assets and debts prior to determination of what is a family asset and what is individually owned. Consider how to handle the discovery of hidden assets.

2. Valuation of defined benefit plans and other assets; security and protection of assets prior to transfer.

3. Division of family assets; discussion of tax issues of asset transfer, and how and when transfers will be accomplished.

4. Division of personal property such as furniture, art, and collectables, tools, and hobby equipment.

5. Handling and division of family debts.

6. Handling of joint bank accounts until assets are divided.

7. Custody arrangement for children; passports.

8. Parenting plan; any special conditions regarding visitation; holidays and special-days arrangements.

9. Child support arrangements; definition of special expenses, and discussion of how these will be paid for; higher education costs and how these will be shared; medical care for children.

10. Tax issues concerning children, such as who claims deductions or credits.

11. Life and disability insurance policies to protect child support in case of death or long-term illness.

12. Estate obligations for child support if no insurance policy in place.

13. Child- or spousal-abuse issues and restraining orders.

14. Personal bankruptcy or protection in case the other spouse goes bankrupt.

15. Spousal support: amount, timeframe, conditions that may cause change to spousal support.

16. Procedure and requirements for change in spousal or child support.

17. Provision for handling disputes if one party does not live up to his or her obligations; penalties such as interest on arrears.

18. Handling of professional fees related to the divorce.

19. Making new wills and power of attorney.

20. Impact and practicality of name change.

After your divorce is final, go over this checklist again to see which items need follow up to ensure that the actions are completed in a proper manner. For example, make sure the joint accounts really are closed; don't just stop using them. If you don't make sure that they are closed, any bad checks written on those accounts will show up on *your* credit report. Be pro-active. One idea is to get a copy of your credit report to ensure that only your debts and obligations are showing on your report. You can do this online, or you can write to the credit bureau requesting a copy. You would normally need to provide copies of two pieces of identification. If there are any joint debts still showing on the report, get it changed immediately. Don't wait until it becomes a problem.

If you are changing your name, change your identification before you change your checks, or at least do not start using the new checks until you have new identification in place. Change everything! It is amazing how many people will change their driver's licenses but not their social security number.

Child Support and Enforcement Resources

United States of America

Administration for Children and Families
370 L'Enfant Promenade, SW
Washington, DC 20201

Federal Office of Child Support Enforcement
www.acf.hhs.gov/programs/cse/

This site has a great deal of information on the state systems and links to each of the states.

Office of Children's Issues
1-888-407-4747
http://travel.state.gov/child_support.html

Information on child support enforcement for international cases.

Canada

British Columbia
British Columbia Ministry of Attorney General Child Support
   Information
British Columbia (other than Vancouver)   1-888-216-2211
Vancouver   (604) 660-2192
www.ag.gov.bc.ca/family-justice/law/child/index.htm

British Columbia adopted the Federal Child Support Guidelines
with minor amendments under its Family Relations Act on April 14,
1998.

Alberta
Edmonton Family Law Information Center   (780) 415-0404
Calgary Family Law Information Center   (403) 297-6600
Toll-free access from other areas within Alberta   310-0000
Alberta Justice Department
www.gov.ab.ca/iust/lawu/roles 13.html
Alberta does not have provincial guidelines. The Federal Child
Support Guidelines apply in cases under the Divorce Act.

Saskatchewan
Saskatchewan Justice Child Support Information   1-888-218-2822
www.saskjustice.gov.sk.ca/Family_Law/Services/toc.shtml

Saskatchewan adopted the Federal Child Support Guidelines under
its Family Maintenance Act as of May 1, 1997.

Manitoba
Manitoba Department of Justice (Family Law)
Manitoba (other than Winnipeg)   1-800-282-8069 ext. 0268
Winnipeg   (204) 945-0268
www.gov.mb.ca/justice/family/familyindex.html

Manitoba adopted child support guidelines under its Family
Maintenance Act on June 1, 1998. The Manitoba guidelines also
apply to cases under the Divorce Act where both parents reside
in Manitoba

Ontario

Ministry of Attorney General
Ontario   1-800-980-4962
www.attorneygeneral.jus.gov.on.ca/html/family/childsptguide-
lines.htm

Ontario adopted the Federal Child Support Guidelines with minor amendments under its Family Law Act on December 1, 1997.

Quebec

Communication Quebec   1-800-363-1363
Quebec Justice Department   (418) 643-5140
www.justice.gouv.qc.ca/english/publications/generale/
modele-a.htm
(Quebec Ministère de la Justice Child Support Information)

The Province of Quebec has provincial guidelines that came into force May 1, 1997. The Quebec guidelines also apply to cases under the Divorce Act where both parents reside in Quebec.

New Brunswick

New Brunswick Department of Justice   1-888-236-2444
http://www.gnb.ca/0062/fsos/index-e.asp

New Brunswick adopted child support guidelines under its Family Services Act on May 1, 1998. The New Brunswick guidelines also apply to cases under the Divorce Act where both parents reside in New Brunswick.

Nova Scotia

Nova Scotia (other than Halifax)   1-800-665-9779
Halifax   (902) 424-4030
Department of Justice
www.gov.ns.ca/just/index.html

Nova Scotia adopted the Federal Child Support Guidelines with minor amendments under its Family Maintenance Act on August 31, 1998.

Prince Edward Island

Prince Edward Island
  (other than Charlottetown)   1-800-240-9798
Charlottetown   (902) 892-0853
http://www.gov.pe.ca/courts/supreme/notes/note9.pdf

PEI adopted the Federal Child Support Guidelines with minor amendments on November 27, 1997. Prince Edward Island's guidelines also apply to cases under the Divorce Act where both parents reside in Prince Edward Island.

Newfoundland and Labrador

Newfoundland & Labrador
Department of Justice   (709) 729-1831
www.gov.nf.ca/just/

Newfoundland adopted the Federal Child Support Guidelines with minor amendments under its Family Law Act on April 1, 1998.

Northwest Territories

Northwest Territories   1-888-298-7880
Yellowknife   (867) 873-7044

Callers should indicate that they would like to speak to someone regarding the Federal Child Support Guidelines.

Government of the Northwest Territories
http://www.gov.nt.ca

The NWT adopted the Federal Child Support Guidelines with minor amendments under its Children 's Law Act on November 1, 1998.

Nunavut

Nunavut (other than Iqaluit)   1-888-298-7880
Iqaluit   (867) 975-6137

Nunavut adopted the Federal Child Support Guidelines with minor amendments under its Children 's Law Act on April 1, 2000.

Yukon
Government of Yukon
Yukon
Whitehorse
www.gov.yk.ca/

1-800-661-0408 ext 3066
(867) 667-3066

Yukon adopted the Federal Child Support Guidelines with minor amendments under its Family Property and Support Act as of April 1, 2000.